FRESH

FROM THE

FARMERS'

MARKET

TITLE:

FRESH FROM THE FARMERS' MARKET

52955

BY: **JANET FLETCHER**

YEAR-ROUND RECIPES FOR THE PICK OF THE CROP

PHOTOGRAPHS BY VICTORIA PEARSON

INTRODUCTION BY ALICE WATERS

CHRONICLE BOOKS

SAN FRANCISCO

This Chronicle Books LLC edition published in 2008.

ISBN 978-0-8118-6590-6

The Library of Congress has cataloged the previous edition as
follows:

Fletcher, Janet Kessel.
   Fresh from the farmers' market: year-round recipes for the
pick of the crop/by Janet Fletcher; introduction by Alice
Waters; photographs by Victoria Pearson.
     p. cm.
   Includes bibliographical references and index.
   ISBN 0-8118-1393-2 (pbk.)
   1. Cookery (Vegetables) 2. Cookery (Fruits) 3. Vegetables.
4. Fruit. I. Title.

TX801.F5597 1997
641.6'5—dc20   96-44631
                       CIP

Manufactured in China.

Food styling by Janet Miller
Designed by Ph.D

10 9 8 7 6 5 4 3

Chronicle Books LLC
680 Second Street
San Francisco, California 94107

www.chroniclebooks.com

FOR DOUG, *sous-chef nonpareil*

CONTENTS

introduction

Thirty-five years ago, in an old house in Berkeley, California, some of my friends and I founded a restaurant we named Chez Panisse. We were driven by a vision of ideal meals prepared from the very best ingredients obtainable, a vision shaped by my experience as a young student in France, where, for the first time in my life, I had seen ordinary people shopping, cooking, and eating as if these activities mattered a great deal more than they seemed to in the suburban America where I had grown up. For my French friends, decisions about food were enormously important; and all around us there were exciting decisions to be made: small, artisanal bakeries and serious butchers and *charcuteries* could still be found in almost every neighborhood; restaurants maintained a quality of service and cooking that was deeply rooted in a tradition of fresh, seasonal food; and, most of all, in cities and towns throughout France people shopped at marketplaces where local produce could be bought directly from its producers.

Back in the supermarkets of California, I despaired of ever finding the same immediacy and aliveness in the food. But we were persistent and gradually expanded our horizons, successfully locating more and more small-scale, local organic farmers and ranchers whose products, at their best, are entirely the equal of the fresh fruits and vegetables I remember from France. Although we were not alone in gravitating toward such purveyors, I like to think that we helped contribute to the creation of a critical mass of consumers hungry for pure and fresh food straight from the source, because there is now a thriving farmers' market in Berkeley, where many of the same farms we buy from have stands.

To my way of thinking, the proliferation of farmers' markets is the single most important and heartening development in this country in my lifetime. Janet Fletcher explains why in this book: farmers' markets bring us the greatest variety of the freshest, tastiest, and most beautiful food there is, food that is neither wastefully packaged, cosmetically waxed, nor irradiated; they bring us the greatest variety and let us taste before we buy; they protect the local environment by sustaining and restoring greenbelts around our cities; and, above all, they build real community by fostering economic and social ties between producers and consumers and by reacquainting us with the agrarian virtues that were once at the heart of our democracy.

In his recent impassioned defense of farming, *Fields without Dreams*, the farmer and classicist Victor Davis Hanson dismisses farmers' markets as "the agricultural equivalents of petting zoos and theme parks" (although he does concede that "genuine agrarians" may be found there). It is true that shopping at farmers' markets cannot alone reverse the decline of family farming, but surely the more we insist on patronizing such markets and the more our diet consists of the food we buy there, the more we will increase the demand for the fruits of a healthier, more humane agriculture.

This book is a straightforward, commonsense, and reliable introduction to the market, and it will guide you in the kitchen, too. Janet cooked at Chez Panisse in the 1980s. Based on the evidence of these pages, her thoroughness, efficiency, and exuberance in the kitchen are all intact. Like me, Janet believes that the most important stylistic element of cooking is always the quality of the ingredients. With her, I hope this book will send you immediately to your farmers' market, willing and eager to let the farmers' market determine what you are going to cook.

ALICE WATERS

off to the market

Every Saturday morning in summer, several thousand people do their food shopping at a lively farmers' market on the San Francisco waterfront. They sample juicy local peaches, sniff plump blackberries, compare the merits of vendors' vine-ripe tomatoes, and watch in delight as a farmer peels back the husk on an ear of white corn to show its perfection. Eventually they head back to their home kitchens, canvas bags and willow baskets bulging with peak-season produce.

Around the country, similar scenes play out each week at the nation's nearly forty-five hundred farmers' markets, a number that has more than doubled since this book was first published in 1997. Tired of mass-produced food and sterile supermarket settings, more people are discovering the pleasure of buying direct from the grower. Farmers' markets have grown exponentially over the past two decades, a reflection of the public's desire for food that is fresher, tastier, and possibly safer. City dwellers have seen markets revitalize downtowns and build an old-fashioned sense of community in urban areas. For customers of Manhattan's Greenmarkets or the twice-weekly Marin County, California, market, shopping is a weekend highlight.

In some parts of the nation, the markets stay open year-round, changing aspect with the changing seasons. The vivid yellows, reds, and greens of summer give way to burgundy, forest green, and burnt orange in autumn as the market fills with butternut and acorn squashes, persimmons, and apples. In winter's white light, farmers with mitten-covered hands sell rutabagas and parsnips, wild mushrooms, broccoli rabe, and thick, sturdy bouquets of kale and collards. Spring paints the market green, the farmers' booths filling with asparagus, artichokes, leeks, peas, fava beans, and herbs.

The advantages of shopping at a farmers' market are clear to anyone who visits one regularly. Other shoppers' motivations may differ, but I can tell you why I prefer to spend my food dollars at a farmers' market.

In my experience, you can't find fresher food unless you grow it yourself. Many growers harvest for a farmers' market the day before, even hours before. In contrast, produce or wholesaler, then to the supermarket's warehouse before it ever makes it to the retail produce department. One government study estimates that the nation's fruits and vegetables travel an average of 1,300 miles before reaching the consumer.

If you care about quality and nutrition, freshness matters. In the hours and days after harvest, produce undergoes change, almost all undesirable. Immediately, moisture begins to evaporate. Cucumbers lose their crisp crunch; basil wilts; peppers and eggplants start to shrivel. Decay sets in, especially on delicate banded produce like lettuce and spinach. And natural sugars in some vegetables begin converting to starch, which is why peas, beets, corn and carrots never taste sweeter than the day they're picked.

Nutrients also dissipate quickly. Broccoli loses 34 percent of its vitamin C in just two days. Asparagus making the refrigerated trek from California to New York arrives with only about one-third of its initial vitamin C.

Growers who sell to supermarkets can't do anything about the nutrients, but some do try to combat moisture loss: they wax the produce. Waxes on cucumbers, peppers, rutabagas, melons, citrus, apples and other fruits and vegetables keep moisture in and give the produce a shiny appearance. According to Bryan Jay Bashin, writing in the magazine *Harrowsmith*, the wax is sometimes mixed with fungicides and sprouting inhibitors before it's applied. The only ways to get rid of it are to scrub your vegetables with detergent or to peel them, which eliminates even more nutrients. A better solution is to buy from farmers' markets, where growers sell their produce too fast to have to bother with waxes.

What's more, the farmers' market offers variety unmatched by the supermarket. In season, I may find 20 different tomato varieties among the growers at a farmers' market, or a dozen different apples or a half-dozen different cucumbers. Supermarkets value uniformity; farmers' markets encourage diversity.

"The farmers' market has been a tremendous vehicle for new-product introduction," confirms Kathleen Barsotti of Capay Fruits & Vegetables in Capay, California. Growers like Barsotti are much more willing to experiment with less-familiar produce items like fava beans or with untried tomato varieties because they can count on the farmers' market as an outlet. "I know I can sell it at the farmers' market if it tastes good," says Barsotti. "At the wholesale market, if people don't recognize it, they don't care how it tastes because they know they can't sell it."

heirloom varieties

In many cases, the experimental seeds that growers are planting are from century-old varieties known as heirlooms. Until farmers' markets gave growers an excuse to grow them, many of these heirlooms were in danger of extinction because they didn't meet the needs of commercial growers. Perhaps they didn't grow uniformly, or didn't ship well, or didn't yield enough—all concerns of farmers who sell their produce to supermarkets. But these antique varieties often have flavor superior to that of the "improved" varieties that replaced them. At farmers' markets, where flavor matters, vendors are reviving these heirlooms, such as Brandywine tomatoes and New England Soldier beans. By purchasing them, I know I am helping preserve a more diverse gene pool—an essential foundation of a healthy, sustainable agriculture system.

Another advantage of farmers' market shopping is getting to taste before you buy. Growers are proud of their produce and pleased to have you try their peaches or pears. In fact, they depend on sampling to help sell unfamiliar apple varieties or plums that taste better than they look. As I sample growers' tomatoes or cucumbers, I'm also gathering ideas for what to try in my own garden. And I find it a real benefit to be able to taste the peaches or apricots before I invest in large quantities for preserves.

I also relish the opportunity to talk directly with growers at the farmers' market, an exchange that never occurs at the supermarket. A grower can point you to the right potatoes for potato salad or the best apples for applesauce. Many farmers are a rich source of recipes and preparation tips. And if you ask, some will happily give you, or sell at a deep discount, the blemished fruit they can't sell at full price—fruit that's perfectly fine for jam, for example. If you are concerned about growing practices and the use of chemical sprays, you can get the answer from the source. The information I get from chatting with growers also makes me a better vegetable gardener.

For city dwellers like myself, farmers' markets bring yet more benefits. By buying direct from the farms that trade at my local markets, I am supporting the outlying greenbelt that makes life in my urban region more pleasurable. Without the farmers' market revival, many of these small farms would now be condominiums or shopping malls. Having the farms nearby not only enriches my dinner table, but also enormously enhances restaurant dining in the San Francisco Bay Area.

community ties

Just as important, farmers' market shopping has become a social activity that connects people with their community. Like the town square or village green of earlier times, the farmers' market provides a place to congregate. One friend tells me that in her small town, everyone meets at the coffee shops near the farmers' market on Sunday morning to have breakfast before or after shopping. I can count on running into friends when I visit the waterfront market in San Francisco or the Jack London Square market in Oakland, and I often see couples, friends, or families with young children happily strolling the market together. A coordinator for Manhattan's Greenmarkets once boasted to me that his markets produced more smiles per square foot than any retail space in New York City. In contrast, supermarket shopping is almost always a solitary experience, or an unpleasant experience shared by a parent and a cranky child.

Budget-conscious buyers can save money at a farmers' market (although I don't always save money; around beautiful produce, I have poor self-control). Because growers who sell at farmers' markets don't have to package or label their produce, or meet industry size and appearance standards, they can pass some of the savings on to consumers. And at some farmers' markets, they do. In my experience, however, farmers at markets in upper-income communities tend to ask what they think their well-heeled audience will pay. To save money, it may pay to compare markets in your region. But even if your purchases are no less expensive than at a supermarket, their quality will almost certainly be superior.

of several Northern California markets, farmers' market shoppers realize the best savings on flowers and organic produce. Other items may be no less expensive than at a supermarket, but the quality will generally be superior.

In addition, many farmers' markets offer more and better organic or unsprayed produce than I can find at conventional markets, and at better prices. Supermarkets rarely have a good selection of organic produce because their shoppers, seeking rock-bottom prices and picture-perfect fruits and vegetables, don't demand it. For many organic farmers, the farmers' market provides a warmer reception.

For shoppers, farmers' markets restore a sense of the seasons, a sense that supermarkets have all but erased. Thanks to imports and controlled storage, you can get just about anything just about anytime at a conventional grocery store. But this year-round "abundance" robs us of the seasonal excitement that comes with the first local strawberries or summer corn. "One of the things that's frustrating is that people are not aware of the seasons," says Debbie Hurley, a California tree-fruit grower. "They don't know when is the right time to be buying certain fruit. There's no awareness of whether it's local or imported. And that's the neat thing about farmers' market customers. They're a lot more aware of those things and willing to devote time to get a superior product."

I've come to believe that anticipation is the secret ingredient in many dishes. When we can have anything we want whenever we want it, nothing seems special. You may only be able to buy corn for a few weeks at your local farmers' market, but it will be tastier for having waited for it.

shopping the market

The typical supermarket shopper makes a list beforehand, then starts at one end of the store and works toward the other. Successful farmers' market shopping requires a different protocol. Here are my thoughts on how to take maximum advantage of what a farmers' market has to offer:

Don't go with a firm shopping list. You may have ideas about dishes you want to prepare in the next few days, but try to be flexible. It's wiser to plan menus once you get to the market and see what's best. It would be a shame to pass up baby beets or impeccable chard because they weren't on your list.

Make the rounds before you buy anything. See who has what, and at what price and quality. Taste and compare different vendors' peaches or melons. Then make your selections, secure in the knowledge that you won't find tastier and cheaper fruit at another stand.

Buy something you haven't tried before. A farmers' market is a great place to get educated about food, if you make the effort. Never cooked kohlrabi? At the farmers' market, a grower can advise you on how to select and prepare it.

Take your own canvas bags, net bags or baskets. Farmers' markets rarely provide shopping carts. Wide woven baskets are ideal because tender fruits and vegetables don't get piled on one another. As you add to your purchases, make sure to shift the heavy items to the bottom. To avoid squashed berries and flattened tomatoes, I like to shop with several canvas bags so there's never too much in any one.

Plan to go straight home after your shopping expedition so you can put away your purchases. Don't leave ripe berries, sweet corn, tender spinach—or anything, for that matter—sweltering in the hot trunk of your car. The heat will quickly suck all the life out of them. If you can't go home right away, bring a cooler for the most delicate items.

Try not to overbuy—my Achilles' heel. One of the main reasons to shop at a farmers' market is to get fresh food. If you let it sit in your refrigerator for days, it won't be fresh any longer. If you buy some items that need to be eaten in the next two or three days, buy other, less perishable foods that will carry you through the end of the week or until your next trip to the market.

Take your children with you. Too many kids have no idea where food comes from or how it looks in its unprocessed state. Seeing zucchini with blossoms attached, carrots with tops or cauliflower with its green wrapper leaves gives them an idea of how vegetables grow. Sampling a half-dozen tomatoes or selecting a peach will awaken their senses. Chances are that youngsters who get to select some of the produce at the farmers' market and talk with the growers will be more adventuresome eaters.

For the best selection and quality, shop early. Growers often bring just a few pounds of something, and naturally, the choice produce goes first. Especially on warm days, the quality of unrefrigerated fruits and vegetables can decline from morning to afternoon. On the other hand, if it's a good price you're after, shop late in the sales day when growers are more inclined to deal.

Take time to chat with farmers. Building relationships is part of the fun of shopping a farmers' market. You will soon become a wiser shopper, probably improve your cooking skills and perhaps take home an occasional "special customer" treat.

using this book

In the following pages, you will find a wide variety of recipes inspired by the farmers' market, including appetizers, soups, salads, pasta, pizza, main courses and desserts. Each of the four seasonal chapters opens with an introduction to the fruits and vegetables you are likely to find in farmers' markets at that time. You will learn how to recognize quality in that particular fruit or vegetable, how to store it and how to use it. Following each seasonal glossary, you will find a list of the recipes in that chapter, organized alphabetically by the dish's dominant fruit or vegetable. I have organized the recipes in this fashion to encourage you to let the market inspire you. If you find beautiful asparagus or perfect peaches, for example, you can quickly locate a recipe that makes the most of your purchase.

Given the nature of agriculture, however, fruits and vegetables rarely fall neatly into one season. In many areas, fennel is a fall crop, planted in mid to late summer. But in mild climates, it can be grown almost year-round. Similarly, where summers get hot, farmers grow beets in spring and fall. Yet I find lovely beets at my local markets in summer, grown on cool, coastal farms.

So to deal with this slippery business of seasons, I have made some assumptions about when fruits and vegetables are likely to be at their best in most areas. For items that straddle seasons or are available much of the year, I've placed them in the seasonal chapter that corresponds, I believe, to when they are most inviting. The citrus harvest, for example, extends well into spring, but I find grapefruits, oranges and their relatives most appealing on winter menus.

Nevertheless, you will find that I don't draw these boundaries strictly. I use leeks (from the winter chapter) in a summer Grand Aioli (page 110) because, in fact, I can find nice leeks in summer. And I am aware that, in some parts of the country, there are few winter or spring markets at all. If farmers' markets operate only from May to October in your region, you should still find this an informative book whose recipes are valid for your more compressed harvest season. And whether you are a six-month or year-round farmers' market patron, I hope these recipes will motivate you to shop your local market more often.

MIXED
SALAD GREENS
.50 bunch
MAKE YOUR OWN
MESCLUN MIX !

spring

Spring arrives at the farmers' market on a wave of green. First come young garlic shoots with their pale green shanks, followed by asparagus spears, standing soldierlike in upright bunches. Soon there's green at every turn: plump artichokes with fresh, moist stems; heaps of English peas; velvet-skinned fava beans and ivory cauliflowers wrapped in green veils. Growers cut avocados into unctuous yellow-green slices for sampling, or refill tubs of hand-cut spring salad mix. Beets, carrots, radishes and turnips show off lush leafy green tops, a sure sign that the roots were recently dug. And bunches of spinach with pink-tipped stems beckon nutrition-conscious shoppers with the rich nutrients in their deep green leaves.

After months of winter citrus, market customers pounce on the first spring strawberries. In the ensuing weeks, the berries' flavor and aroma will improve, spurring even reluctant cooks into the kitchen to make strawberry shortcake, a strawberry tart, tapioca with strawberry-rhubarb sauce or strawberry jam. By late spring, tree-ripened apricots and cherries have begun their brief run, offering farmers' market shoppers an extraordinary eating experience that too few Americans have.

apricots

Tree-ripened apricots—the only kind worth eating—rarely make it to a supermarket. They are simply too fragile and too dependent on special handling to survive the trip. "For supermarkets, you have to pick apricots almost green," says Ignacio Sanchez, who grows them at his Twin Girls Farm in Reedley, California. For farmers' markets, he cultivates varieties prized for taste—such as Earlicots, Pattersons and Blenheims—and leaves them on the tree to develop color and sweetness. If picked at the proper moment, the Blenheim in particular has the perfume, the sweet-tart balance and the soft, juicy texture that apricot lovers seek.

selection: First, check for that characteristic apricot aroma. The fruit should be well colored and have some give when gently pressed. Stay away from apricots with green-tinged shoulders; they were picked too soon.

storage: Store at room temperature or refrigerate if fully ripe.

artichokes

Most artichokes love cool, foggy weather, which is why they thrive along California's midcoast. If you drive the coast route between San Francisco and Monterey, you may spot vast silvery stands of artichokes around Pescadero and Castroville, the large, prickly plants looking like they could yield nothing edible. But in early spring, and to a lesser extent in the fall, the plants produce the plump flower buds that we eat.

Market shoppers will find artichokes in a wide range of sizes. Size has nothing to do with maturity; it indicates where the bud was on the plant. The baby artichokes are at the base of the plant, among the fronds, where they get little sun. Trimmed and thinly sliced, they are tender enough to eat raw with olive oil and lemon. The bigger specimens are more exposed. In small or medium artichokes, the peeled stem can be delicious—another reason to shop at the farmers' market, where the freshly harvested artichokes often have at least an inch of stem attached.

selection: Marcia Muzzi, who grows artichokes in Pescadero, California, advises market shoppers to use the "squeak test": a fresh artichoke will squeak when you rub it between your fingers. (Thornless varieties—so-called because they don't have prickly tips—don't squeak, however.) They should also feel firm and heavy for their size, which indicates they still have a lot of moisture, and the stem should look freshly cut. The best artichokes are tightly closed, with no bruising or darkening. But don't pass up artichokes with leaves that have a bronzed, blistery look. Those have been "frost-kissed," the growers say; they may be the ugliest but, for reasons even the farmers don't understand, they taste the best.

storage: Keep artichokes in a closed plastic bag in the refrigerator crisper, with a few drops of water in the bag to keep them moist.

asparagus

Each spring, when straight, slender green spears begin to push their way out of the ground, an asparagus bed looks like a miniature tree farm. At any given time, the bed will have spears of widely varying lengths, so harvesters have to pass through frequently, using a special tool to cut the spears at ground level. And the warmer the weather, the faster they grow—as much as four inches a day when nights are warm, says California grower Stan Cutter. In the warmest growing regions, harvesters have to go through a bed twice a day.

A few growers are now producing white asparagus, so prized in Europe. It is not a different variety but the same plant, grown under mulch or a plastic cover so the spears never see sun. Cutter believes they are sweeter than the green spears; I find them less flavorful. He also grows a purple variety that is tender enough to eat raw in salads; the spears turn green when cooked.

selection: Asparagus breaks down rapidly after harvest, losing sugar and moisture. "Look at the butt," advises Cutter. "If it's shriveled and dry, you know it's old." The spears should be green from tip to butt, with little or no white. Size isn't a sign of age or quality. Skinny spears tend to come from new beds and old beds; a bed in its prime will produce mostly stout spears.

storage: Refrigerate in a plastic bag. If you need to keep them for more than a day or two and they seem a little limp, rehydrate them by cutting the ends and standing them in an inch or so of water in the refrigerator for an hour.

avocados

Growers who are first in the market with a crop are usually rewarded with a high price, although the early harvest is rarely the best. California avocados are a good example. The longer they stay on the tree, the more oil they develop, and oil content determines flavor. That's why Bud Weisenberg, a grower who sells at farmers' markets, stalls his harvest as long as possible. With some varieties, he starts picking as much as two months after his industry colleagues.

Another factor contributes to his fruit's superior quality. "The avocados you see at a supermarket go in and out of refrigerated trucks and cold rooms all the time," says Weisenberg. And that's not good. "Any time you put fruit in the refrigerator, it affects the flavor." His own avocados go from tree to box to truck to farmers' market. "They never see a cold room," he says.

selection: California's premium avocado is the pebbly-skinned Hass, the latest-maturing variety and the one with the highest oil content. Picked and sold firm, the Hass is ready to eat when the skin turns black and the flesh gives to gentle pressure. The Fuerte, a thin-skinned green-when-ripe avocado, is best in early spring. Picked hard, it will ripen at room temperature and develop fine flavor. You may also occasionally see tiny "cocktail avocados" at the market; these are not a separate variety but miniature pit-free fruits that develop, inexplicably, on the same tree. Florida, California's avocado rival, grows mostly smooth-skinned, green-when-ripe varieties. Compared to California fruit, these avocados are high in water content and low in oil. They are suitable for slicing in salads but lack the richness required for a good guacamole or other Mexican dishes.

Avocados should be firm when purchased, unless you plan to eat them immediately. They should feel heavy for their size, which indicates high oil content. Large avocados aren't necessarily more flavorful, but they tend to be a better buy because they have a higher proportion of flesh to pit.

storage: Ripen avocados at room temperature until they give to gentle pressure. To speed up the process, put the avocados in a paper bag in a warm place, such as on top of the refrigerator. Or put in a fruit bowl with any other fruits; the ethylene gas they emit will help ripen the avocados. Eat when ripe. Don't try to extend their life by refrigerating them, which deadens their flavor.

beets

If you shopped only at a supermarket, you might never know that beets could be other than round and red. But farmers' market customers enjoy enticing variety, choosing from red, golden, candy-striped and even white beets. They can sometimes buy beets an inch in diameter and as sweet as candy, or cylindrical roots that make uniform slices from one end to the other, perfect for pickling.

They can also count on finding beets with their nutritious greens attached, which, says California grower Dru Rivers, is half the reason to buy beets. In grocery stores, produce managers remove the greens when they begin to decay; they would not only be unattractive, but would also signal that the beets weren't fresh. You can steam or boil the greens as you do spinach or chard, removing the stems if they are tough.

selection: More important than size is freshness. "Beets are a lot like sweet corn," explains Rivers. "They're best when eaten right after they're picked because their sugar starts to turn to starch. We always pick ours the day before the farmers' market. I don't think you ever find that at the supermarket." For proof of freshness, examine the greens.

storage: Separate the roots from the greens if you are going to store your beets more than a day or two. Store roots and greens separately in open plastic bags in the refrigerator crisper.

carrots

There's a reason why most supermarkets sell only "clip-top" carrots—carrots with the greens removed. The tops are a mark of freshness. The bagged and bulk carrots may be weeks or months old, but with no greens to guide you, you can't know. But you can taste the difference: although carrots keep relatively well, a freshly pulled carrot will be sweeter and juicier than a stored one, and more nutritious, too.

Mary Ann Carpenter, a Southern California grower, says her farmers' market customers want to see the tops. They know that there are few other visual clues to quality. "I don't think you really can judge by appearance," says Carpenter. Firm, shapely, bright orange carrots don't always taste great; misshapen carrots—the result of growing in rocky soil—can be delicious. You have to "taste around" at the market to find the farmer whose carrots are sweetest.

Knowing they have an adventuresome audience, growers who sell at the farmers' market often try a lot of different varieties. In addition to the familiar long, tapered roots, you may found short, fat ones; round ones; giant ones (that are nonetheless sweet); and, of course, slender baby carrots that are perfect for children. By buying these less common varieties, you encourage farmers to expand their selections and help keep alive a broad range of choices.

selection: Let the tops be your guide: they should be bright green and fresh looking. If they aren't attached, inspect the stem end for the darkening that indicates age. Old carrots also tend to produce little hairlike roots.

storage: Remove the greens before storing; they draw moisture from the carrots. Store the carrots in a closed plastic bag, preferably the sturdy, store-bought type with a top closure. Carrots get limp when exposed to air.

cauliflower

The smooth, creamy white face of a cauliflower is like an old-time southern belle's: both owe their beauty to constant protection from the sun's browning rays. Some cauliflower varieties are self-blanching, with a wrapper of light green leaves. Others must be forcibly blanched by tying the leaves around the maturing head with a rubber band.

Cauliflower is easier to grow to perfection in cool weather. In hot weather, the vegetable's cap of sheltering green leaves will quickly open, and the head will yellow or develop brown splotches and separate into florets. The ideal cauliflower grows slowly and is picked just when the wrapper leaves begin to pull away (if it hasn't been forcibly blanched).

selection: Look for a creamy white curd that's tight and smooth. If it's discolored or starting to open into florets, the cauliflower will probably have what produce people call a "ricey" texture and a stronger, more cabbagelike flavor. You may also see green- or purple-heading cauliflower at the farmers' market. The flavor is similar to the white variety; again, look for tightly clustered curds. Size doesn't matter.

storage: Take your cauliflower home from the farmers' market and eat it that night, recommends grower Andy Griffin of California's Happy Boy Farms. Cauliflower will last several days in the refrigerator in a plastic bag, but it will never taste better than the day you buy it. "People are always coming and telling me how long something lasted," says Griffin, "and I think, 'Why?' Eat it! One of the nicest things about farmers' markets, to my mind, is the possibility of getting something fresh. If you buy it fresh but sit on it for a week, you've lost the best thing it had."

cherries

In late spring, during the few weeks cherries dominate the farmers' market, I don't think many people leave without some. "Once the cherries show up at my booth, I can't sell anything else," one grower complained to me. Lines form as shoppers painstakingly pick the fattest, ripest cherries out of the farmers' wooden bins, and around the market, you see people relishing the quintessential hand-to-mouth fruit.

Most people agree that the Bing is the king of sweet cherries—large, meaty, sweet and firm. Early cherries, like Black Tartarian and Burlat, keep us satisfied until the Bings arrive; yellow cherries such as Royal Anne and Rainier look beautiful in a fruit bowl and can be tasty, but there's nothing like a perfect sweet-tart Bing. For pies and jam and for drying, most people prefer a sour cherry, such as Montmorency or English Morello.

selection: Color is the main sign that a cherry is ripe and ready for harvest. Growers whose goal is flavor, not shippability, leave cherries on the tree until they are 95 to 100 percent scarlet red (for red varieties). For yellow varieties, look for large, evenly yellow fruit with a red blush. Cherries should be firm, not soft, and have a nice sheen. A green stem indicates a fresh-picked cherry.

storage: Refrigerate cherries in a plastic bag. Don't wash them until you are ready to eat them.

fava beans

For years, if you wanted fava beans in San Francisco, you had to hang around one of the Italian markets in North Beach. If you spotted the beans, you had to move fast, before the neighborhood's older Italian ladies found them, too. Now Italians aren't the only ones sifting through the mounds of fat green pods that are increasingly showing up at farmers' markets. American chefs and home cooks eager to make traditional Mediterranean dishes are discovering the appeal of these tender, fresh shelling beans.

For most preparations, fava beans should be double-peeled: You have to shell them like English peas, then you need to remove each bean's thick skin. (It's not that onerous. See page 46 for peeling instructions.) Add peeled favas to tomato- or olive oil-based pasta sauces, to risottos and rice pilafs with other spring vegetables, and to vegetable soups and stews. Italians serve the shelled but unpeeled young beans as an appetizer with cubes of pecorino cheese, with diners peeling their own beans or not, as they like.

selection: Fava bean pods should be unblemished, somewhat shiny and velvety to the touch; dull-looking pods were not recently picked. You should be able to feel the individual beans inside the pod; for the sweetest beans, choose pods where the beans are fully formed but on the small side. Like peas, fava beans quickly convert their natural sugar to starch; if you don't get fresh-picked ones, you may wonder what all the fuss is about.

storage: Plan to use fava beans the day you buy them. If you must store them, refrigerate in a plastic bag.

green garlic

In early to mid-spring, when new garlic plants have sent up their leafy shoots but have not yet formed a bulb, they are a prize in their own right. Harvested at that stage, they look like baby leeks or thick green onions, but one whiff of their slender white shanks gives them away. They are so mild at this point that you can use them with abandon; they contribute a delicate garlic flavor with no trace of heat.

A few weeks later, if left in the ground, the base of each plant will swell into a solid cream-colored bulb with a papery covering. At farmers' markets in late spring, you may also find garlic at this slightly more pungent stage, before the bulb has separated into individual, paper-wrapped cloves. It's a pleasure to use at this point because you don't have to peel each clove, and you can add it liberally without producing a flavor that's sharp or hot. At both stages, green garlic shows best in simple preparations that allow its subtle presence to shine: with scrambled eggs, in mashed potatoes, in brothy soups or with other delicate spring vegetables such as peas, fava beans and asparagus.

selection: Fresh-looking greens guarantee that the garlic was freshly dug. Avoid bunches that show signs of decay; you can peel back the decomposing layers, but then you are paying for something you can't use.

storage: Refrigerate in a plastic bag. Because they are moist and fresh, green garlic shoots will only last about as long as green onions. The young bulbs with unformed cloves will last longer, but you should use them before the refrigerator dries them out.

english peas

Starchy peas must seem like a fact of life to people who buy peas at conventional markets. I have bought many pounds myself, always hoping that careful cooking will somehow improve them.

"The best peas are the ones I eat when I'm checking for weeds," says Northern California grower Larry Jacobs. After harvest, fresh peas quickly convert their sugar to starch, a process that can only be slowed—not stopped—by chilling the peas right away. Even so, says Jacobs, the best determinant of pea taste is "the time between harvest and your mouth."

Jacobs's peas reach a farmers' market within two days; a supermarket pea is likely to be a week old, he says, because it has to pass through a distributor or wholesaler. If you can't grow peas yourself and carry them straight from the vine to the pot, a farmers' market provides your best shot at the kind of peas gardeners rave about.

selection: Even a fresh English pea won't taste good if it was picked too late or too early, says Jacobs. Look for pods that are filled out but not to the point that you can see the shape of the peas. You can ask when the peas were harvested, but you will learn more by asking to sample.

storage: Ideally, you should cook and enjoy your peas the day you buy them. If you must store them, refrigerate in an open plastic bag.

radishes

They may not have much else to take to market in early spring, but growers can count on having radishes. It takes less than 30 days to mature a crop, even during spring's first cool weeks. In fact, radishes prefer a cool growing season, becoming hot in flavor in tandem with the weather.

"The main thing is to pick them when they're still really crunchy," says California grower Dru Rivers. Within a week, they can go from just-right to hot and pithy. Some people like a spicy bite to their radishes, but nobody likes them soft. They are short-lived out of the ground, too; by getting her radishes to the farmers' market the day after harvest, Rivers provides her customers with exceptional radishes that will last a few days in their kitchen.

To garnish hors d'oeuvre platters and salads, look for the elongated French Breakfast radish with its red shoulders and white tip. Easter Egg radishes come in a variety of pastel hues; the different colors are grown and bundled together to make an eye-pleasing bunch. At your farmers' market, you may spot purple radishes, white radishes, cylindrical ones and the familiar round Cherry Belles.

selection: Perky greens are a sure sign that the radishes were freshly picked. The radishes themselves should feel firm and smooth, with few or no cracks. Small ones are likely to be milder and more crisp than large ones.

storage: Remove the greens (they draw out moisture) and refrigerate radishes in an open plastic bag in the crisper. Use within two or three days. If you want to leave the greens on for display, remove any binding band before storing.

rhubarb

It's little wonder that many older cooks and gardeners refer to rhubarb as "pie plant." A double-crust rhubarb pie, with or without strawberries, is perhaps this vegetable's finest moment. Mouth-puckeringly tart when raw, rhubarb blossoms when cooked and sweetened. A strawberry rhubarb sauce or crisp has that fine balance of sweet and sour that makes you crave another bite.

Rhubarb needs winter chill to perform properly in the spring, pushing its celerylike leafy stalks up from an underground tuber. Growers typically harvest the stalks by twisting them loose; cutting them off can cause the ends to curl. After harvest, the leaves are removed (they are toxic) and the stalks are usually chilled before their trip to market. "We harvest the day we're going to sell," says Seattle-area grower Sue Verdi, whose rhubarb goes straight to that city's Pike Place Market. In contrast, adds Verdi, supermarket rhubarb can be weeks old.

Farmers with a hothouse can produce rhubarb year-round. Naturally, hothouse growers claim theirs is more tender, less stringy; producers of field-grown product say theirs is more flavorful and more durable. The bottom line, according to California grower Don Ward: "There's not a heck of a lot of difference."

selection: Depending on the variety, rhubarb can be red, pink, green or speckled. Verdi prefers red varieties, finding them sweeter, but says there's no reason to reject stalks that aren't bright red. They should be crisp, however, and without significant blemishes. Late in the season, large stalks can get a little stringy or pithy; early on, they are likely to be just as tender as small stalks.

storage: Store rhubarb in the refrigerator crisper in an open plastic bag. It wouldn't hurt to wrap the stalks with a damp paper towel to help keep in moisture.

salad greens

Grocery stores have expanded their selection of salad greens in the past few years, even offering the washed and dried mix of baby lettuces widely known as mesclun. But only at the farmers' market will shoppers get a real sense of how rich the greens world is, because many of the tastiest and most beautiful salad greens are too fragile to ship.

Seed catalogs are enticing farmers' market growers with numerous heirloom and hybrid varieties—among them, Rouge d'Hiver, a 150-year-old red romaine; frilly red-tipped Lollo Rosso; the elongated Deer Tongue lettuce; and delicate, lobed Oakleaf. Some are even cultivating miner's lettuce for their adventurous farmers' market customers, a green that grows wild in forest and mountain areas. Others are harvesting *mâche*, also known as corn salad, which has pretty rosette-shaped leaves; in France, bistro patrons enjoy it with sliced beets.

If you can find frisée at the supermarket at all, it is likely to be oversized, tough and bitter. The same goes for escarole. But these are fine salad additions when picked young, as they usually are for the farmers' market. Frisée (curly endive) has tiny white ribs and frilly green tips; it adds texture and a mild bitterness. Escarole, with its broad white ribs and pale yellow-green heart, is a sturdy, pleasantly bitter green with a satisfying crunch.

Many farmers today are bringing baby lettuce mixes to the market, typically in a fresher state than you would find them at the grocery store. "Ours get to the farmers' market the day after they're picked," says Kathleen Barsotti of California's Capay Fruits & Vegetables. Freshness is critical with these baby lettuces because they decline quickly. Barsotti's greens are hand-cut with scissors, mixed according to the farm's recipe, washed repeatedly in big tubs, then spun dry in an electric salad spinner that's almost as big as a washing machine.

selection: Baby lettuce mixes should smell fresh, look perky and have no standing moisture or visible decay. More mature salad greens should be turgid, not limp. It's pretty easy to spot tired salad greens; you should leave them behind.

storage: Discard any damaged outer greens. If there is a band around the head or bunch, remove it. Store unwashed greens in a perforated plastic bag in the refrigerator crisper. You can also wash the greens, spin them dry and then layer them with paper towels. Roll the towels loosely and put in a plastic bag in the refrigerator crisper.

spinach

In cool weather, a spinach seed yields edible returns quickly—in 40 to 50 days, even less for baby spinach. But after rapid growth comes rapid decline; once harvested, spinach doesn't have many good days left.

At a farmers' market, you are likely to find spinach harvested just a day or two before, with fresh, bright, tender leaves that show no sign of decay. Because farmers who grow for the farmers' market don't have to be as concerned about shippability, they can harvest the spinach when it is young, thin stemmed and delicate.

selection: Some spinach varieties have smooth, flat leaves; others, known as Savoy types, have crinkly, thicker leaves. The crinkly leaved types are harder to clean but arguably have more flavor. Whichever type you buy, it should have bright green, crisp leaves with no sign of yellowing or decay. For delicacy of texture and flavor, choose small leaves with thin stems over large leaves with thick stems.

storage: If spinach is bunched when you buy it, undo the band when you get it home. Store loose spinach in an open plastic bag in the vegetable crisper and use as soon as possible.

strawberries

When was the last time a supermarket produce manager offered you a strawberry to sample? At farmers' markets, strawberry growers love to give shoppers a taste because they know they will make a sale: everybody can recognize great-tasting strawberries and few can resist them.

Supermarket berries tend to fall short because they are typically varieties bred to withstand shipping; they must be firm and not very juicy, or they will be strawberry sauce before they reach the consumer. For farmers' markets, growers can select varieties renowned for flavor and pick them fully ripe, knowing that they will get them to the customer within a day.

selection: "A shiny berry is a fresh berry," says Molly Gean, a California strawberry grower. "If the shine is off the berry, it's a good chance it's several days off the plant." An intense perfume also indicates a tasty berry; so does full, red color. Avoid fruit with green tips or with open tips. Always inspect the berries for mold; one moldy berry can quickly ruin others.

storage: If you plan to eat the berries that day, leave them at room temperature. Otherwise, refrigerate them. The secret to extending their life is keeping them dry and airtight, says Gean. She lines a plastic container with paper towels, puts the dry berries in and then tops them with paper towels before sealing the container. Never wash strawberries until you are ready to use them; then wash and dry them quickly.

turnips

Sometimes I find turnips at the farmers' market that aren't much bigger than radishes. They are a prize, with silky-textured roots and greens so tender they need just a quick steaming.

California grower Paul Holmes laughs when people get excited about turnips. To his mother, they were Depression food. Turnips do grow quickly and easily, but they are much more than just a last-resort vegetable. When grown in cool weather and harvested young, sweet turnips and their tops deserve careful treatment. Braise the turnips in butter, pair with peas or cook alongside a pork roast. Steam young greens just until wilted, then toss with the cooked roots; simmer older greens in a flavorful pork broth.

selection: "You can have an awfully big turnip that still tastes great," says Holmes; it depends on the variety and the growing conditions. But in general, small turnips will have a milder flavor and smoother, silkier texture than large ones. The greens, if attached, will tell you whether the roots were freshly dug. Although harvested turnips don't deteriorate rapidly, they do gradually lose moisture, so freshness counts.

storage: If the greens are attached, cut them off, store them separately and use them quickly. Both greens and roots should be stored in plastic bags in the refrigerator crisper.

warm apricot tart

A sliver of fresh apricot tart with a glass of Sauternes strikes me as one of the world's great food and wine marriages. At the farmers' market, look for apricots that are ripe but firm.

FOR THE CRUST:

1 CUP UNBLEACHED ALL-PURPOSE FLOUR
1 TABLESPOON SUGAR
¼ TEASPOON SALT
½ CUP UNSALTED BUTTER, CHILLED, IN SMALL PIECES
1½ TABLESPOONS ICE WATER

FOR THE FILLING:

ICE WATER
1½ POUNDS RIPE APRICOTS
⅓ CUP SUGAR

⅓ CUP STRAINED APRICOT JAM (SEE NOTE)

MAKES ONE 9-INCH TART, TO SERVE 8

NOTE: To make strained jam, heat jam in a small saucepan over low heat, stirring until it thins. Add a few drops of water, if necessary. Using a rubber spatula, push jam through a sieve. Use while still warm.

To make the crust: In a food processor, combine flour, sugar and salt. Pulse three or four times to blend. Add butter and pulse until mixture resembles coarse crumbs. Sprinkle water over mixture and pulse until it just starts to come together. It will be crumbly; do not overwork. Transfer to a sheet of plastic wrap and top with another sheet. Pat and press dough into a flattened square, always pressing with the wrap so that your warm hands don't touch the dough. Wrap tightly in plastic and refrigerate 30 minutes.

Preheat oven to 375 degrees F. Unwrap dough and put it on a work surface between two fresh sheets of plastic wrap. With a rolling pin, flatten dough into an evenly thick circle large enough to cover the bottom and sides of a 9-inch tart tin with a removable bottom. Transfer to the tart tin, removing the bottom piece of plastic wrap. With the top sheet of plastic wrap still in place to keep your hand from touching the dough, press the dough into the tart tin. Remove the plastic. Patch any thin spots with extra dough, then trim dough even with the pan rim. Chill dough 30 minutes. Prick with a fork in several places, then bake until golden, about 25 minutes. Cool on a rack.

Reduce oven heat to 350 degrees F.

To make the filling: Bring a saucepan full of water to a boil over high heat. Have ready a bowl of ice water. Add apricots a few at a time to the boiling water and blanch 15 seconds, then transfer to the ice water to stop the cooking. When cool, lift out and peel the apricots—the skins should slip off easily—halve them and discard pits. Cut each half lengthwise into thirds, or, if quite small, cut in two. Arrange the pieces tightly packed in the tart shell, rounded sides down. Sprinkle with sugar.

Bake until apricots are soft, about 45 minutes. Remove from oven and brush with strained jam. Serve warm.

artichokes roman style with garlic and mint

Mounds of plump artichokes signal the beginning of spring at the farmers' market, a sure sign that asparagus, peas and fava beans won't be far behind. In Rome, cooks trim the artichokes down to the tender, pale part, then braise them whole—pared stem intact—with garlic, parsley, mint and white wine. If you quarter the artichokes before cooking, as I suggest, you can serve them as part of a larger antipasto—with sliced prosciutto, for example, and some black olives. Guests can take just a couple of wedges instead of feeling obliged to eat a whole artichoke.

You have to remove quite a few of the artichoke leaves to reach the tender heart; if you don't remove enough, the braised artichokes will be too tough to eat with knife and fork. But you don't need to discard the tougher leaves. Steam them the next day and enjoy them with garlic mayonnaise.

JUICE OF 1 LEMON

4 LARGE ARTICHOKES, ABOUT 10 OUNCES EACH

½ LEMON

¼ CUP OLIVE OIL

4 CLOVES GARLIC, MINCED

3 SHALLOTS, MINCED

¼ CUP MINCED ITALIAN PARSLEY

3 TABLESPOONS CHOPPED MINT

½ CUP DRY WHITE WINE

1 TEASPOON SALT

FRESHLY GROUND BLACK PEPPER

SERVES 4

Prepare the artichokes: Fill a large bowl with cold water and add lemon juice. Pull back the outer leaves of each artichoke until they break at the base. Continue removing leaves until you reach the pale green, tender inner leaves. Reserve outer leaves for another use (see recipe introduction). With a large, sharp knife, cut about 1 inch off the top of each artichoke; trim the stem, leaving about 1 inch attached. Rub the cut surfaces with the lemon half. With a small knife, pare the stem and the base of each artichoke, removing any dark green parts to reveal the pale yellow-green heart. Quarter each artichoke. With a spoon, scrape out the hairy choke and prickly inner leaves. Immediately place quarters in lemon water to prevent browning.

Heat olive oil in a large skillet over moderate heat. Add garlic, shallots, parsley and mint. Saute about 3 minutes to soften shallots and release garlic fragrance. Drain the artichokes and pat them dry. Add to the skillet along with the wine, the 1 teaspoon salt and the pepper to taste. Toss to coat artichokes with seasonings. Spoon some of the herbal mixture into the hollow of each artichoke quarter, then cover skillet, reduce heat to low and cook until artichokes are tender when pierced with a knife, about 20 minutes.

Remove from heat, uncover and cool to room temperature in skillet. Serve at room temperature.

roasted asparagus

California grower Stan Cutter told me he learned this method of cooking the spears from a farmers' market customer who would buy several pounds from him almost every week. He finally asked her what she was doing with all the asparagus, and she told him she liked to have friends over for roasted asparagus feasts. Prepared this way, they are indeed a feast—simple and good. Roasting seems to intensify their flavor. After trying it, I realized how much flavor I had been throwing out over the years when I tossed out the cooking liquid.

By asparagus "tips" I mean the tender green part remaining when you snap the spear between your hands. Depending on how well trimmed they are at the market, you may need to buy three or four pounds to yield two pounds of tips. In my house, they would be a first course, but you could serve them as an accompaniment to roast lamb or prime rib. For a light supper, top them with poached eggs.

2 POUNDS ASPARAGUS TIPS (WEIGHT AFTER TRIMMING)
¼ CUP EXTRA VIRGIN OLIVE OIL
KOSHER SALT

SERVES 4

Preheat oven to 450 degrees F. Divide asparagus between 2 rimmed baking sheets. Drizzle half of the olive oil over each batch and sprinkle generously with salt. Toss the spears with your hands to coat them evenly with oil and salt, then spread them out so they are in one layer.

Bake until spears are sizzling and just tender, about 10 minutes, switching the position of the trays halfway through. Transfer to a platter and serve immediately.

pappardelle with asparagus and fava beans

It's useful to note that vegetables available in the farmers' market at the same time generally go well together. In spring, you almost can't go wrong mixing asparagus, fava beans, peas, green onions, artichokes and leeks—either in pairs or more elaborate combinations. They share a sweet, tender quality that shows best in simple preparations, such as this dish of buttered wide noodles with asparagus tips, fava beans and prosciutto.

1 POUND FRESH EGG PASTA IN SHEETS

SEMOLINA FLOUR OR UNBLEACHED ALL-PURPOSE FLOUR

2 TABLESPOONS OLIVE OIL

4 TABLESPOONS UNSALTED BUTTER

1 CUP MINCED SHALLOTS

3 OUNCES PROSCIUTTO DI PARMA, MINCED

¼ CUP MINCED ITALIAN PARSLEY

2 CLOVES GARLIC, MINCED

¼ POUND THIN ASPARAGUS TIPS (WEIGHT AFTER TRIMMING), SLICED ON THE DIAGONAL INTO ¼-INCH LENGTHS

SALT AND FRESHLY GROUND BLACK PEPPER

½ CUP HOMEMADE OR CANNED LOW-SODIUM CHICKEN BROTH

1 CUP PEELED FAVA BEANS (SEE PAGE 46), FROM ABOUT 2 POUNDS UNSHELLED FAVA BEANS

By hand, cut the pasta into pappardelle—ribbons about 8 inches long and ¾ inch wide. Dust lightly with semolina or all-purpose flour to keep the noodles from sticking and set aside on a tray.

Heat olive oil and butter in a 12-inch skillet over moderate heat. Add shallots, prosciutto, parsley and garlic and saute until shallots are softened, about 3 minutes. Add asparagus, season well with salt and pepper and toss to coat with seasonings. Add broth, bring to a simmer, cover and adjust heat to maintain a gentle simmer. Cook until asparagus are crisp-tender, 8 to 10 minutes. Add fava beans, cover and continue cooking until beans and asparagus are tender, another 2 minutes or more. Taste and adjust seasoning.

Bring a large pot of salted water to a boil over high heat. Add pasta and cook until al dente. Drain, leaving a little water clinging to the noodles; return noodles to pot. Add sauce and toss gently but well. Serve on warm plates.

SERVES 4 TO 6

asparagus with soft-scrambled eggs

Asparagus growers, like corn growers, say the best way to cook their vegetable is to put the water on to boil before you harvest. Asparagus quickly loses moisture and sugar after picking, so its flavor and texture are compromised. If you don't grow your own, your next best option is to buy your asparagus at a farmers' market where it likely was picked the day before. And if your market has an egg vendor selling fresh-laid eggs, you are in luck. Asparagus and eggs enhance each other, whether it's a fried egg atop buttered asparagus; a soft-cooked egg cut open and used as a dipping sauce for asparagus tips; chopped eggs in the vinaigrette over boiled asparagus; or this combination of creamy soft-scrambled eggs over warm buttered tips. If you want to make the dish more dramatic, shave black truffle over each portion.

1 POUND THIN ASPARAGUS
4 LARGE EGGS
2 TABLESPOONS HEAVY CREAM
2 TABLESPOONS UNSALTED BUTTER
SALT AND FRESHLY GROUND BLACK PEPPER
1 TABLESPOON THINLY SLICED FRESH CHIVES

SERVES 4 AS A FIRST COURSE, 2 AS A LUNCH

Preheat oven to warm. Holding an asparagus spear in both hands, bend it gently; it will break naturally at the point at which the spear becomes tough. Repeat with remaining spears. Set the tender ends aside with all the tips pointing in the same direction; discard the tough ends.

In a small bowl, beat eggs and cream together with a fork.

In a large skillet, bring an inch of salted water to a boil over high heat. Add asparagus, keeping all the tips pointing in the same direction. Boil until just tender, about 2 minutes. Lift asparagus out with tongs and transfer to a clean dish towel. Pat dry. Drain skillet, return the asparagus to the skillet and toss gently with 1 tablespoon butter and salt to taste, taking care to keep the tips pointed in the same direction. Transfer asparagus to a serving platter and place in oven to keep warm.

Melt remaining tablespoon butter in the top of a double boiler set over—not touching— barely simmering water. Add eggs and cook slowly, stirring constantly with a rubber spatula and scraping the sides of the bowl often. You want them to set in a creamy mass, without forming curds. When eggs begin to thicken and set, after 3 to 5 minutes, season with salt and pepper. When they are set but as soft and creamy as a thick béchamel sauce, stir in chives and remove from heat.

Immediately spoon the eggs over the middle of the asparagus spears and serve on warm plates.

penne with green cauliflower, anchovies and bread crumbs

Cauliflower takes a great deal of seasoning, I find, and this Sicilian pasta dish has that—lots of garlic, hot-pepper flakes and anchovies. Use more or fewer anchovies, depending on the size of the ones you buy and how much you like them. The crunchy bread crumbs sprinkled on top take the place of cheese. Of course, you can substitute white cauliflower if there is no green cauliflower at the market. Or use chartreuse broccoli romanesco or even just plain broccoli.

⅓ CUP PLUS 1 TABLESPOON EXTRA VIRGIN OLIVE OIL

1 CUP FINE BREAD CRUMBS (SEE NOTE)

SALT

4 TO 6 ANCHOVY FILLETS, FINELY MINCED

4 CLOVES GARLIC, MINCED

¼ TEASPOON HOT RED PEPPER FLAKES

1 POUND GREEN CAULIFLOWER, PREFERABLY IN ONE PIECE

1 POUND DRIED PENNE OR OREC-CHIETTE

1 TABLESPOON MINCED ITALIAN PARSLEY

SERVES 4 TO 6

NOTE: To make fine bread crumbs, use day-old bread containing only flour, water, yeast and salt. Preheat oven to 300 degrees F. Remove the crusts from the bread; if the bread is unsliced, cut into ½-inch-thick slices. Toast slices on a baking sheet until dry. Cool, then break slices into small pieces and process in a food processor until fine.

Heat 1 tablespoon olive oil in a small skillet over moderately low heat. Add bread crumbs and sauté, stirring often, until they are golden brown, about 10 minutes. Season with salt and set aside.

Heat remaining ⅓ cup olive oil in a large skillet over moderately low heat. Add anchovies, garlic and hot-pepper flakes and sauté slowly a minute or two to release garlic fragrance. Set aside.

Bring a large pot of salted water to a boil over high heat. Add the cauliflower and cook until it is tender but not soft, about 5 minutes, or less if cauliflower is in smaller pieces. Lift out of boiling water, drain, then chop into very small pieces. Transfer to skillet with anchovies and toss to coat with seasonings. Return skillet to moderately low heat, add ⅓ cup hot water from the pasta pot and keep warm.

Add pasta to the same boiling water used to cook the cauliflower. Boil until al dente, then drain. Return pasta to pot and add cauliflower sauce and parsley. Toss well, then divide among warm plates. Top each serving with a tablespoon of the bread crumbs and pass remaining bread crumbs at the table so diners can add them as they eat.

cauliflower and potato soup with cilantro

With no logo-imprinted cellophane wrap to hide its beauty, cauliflower at the farmers' market is an appetizing sight. Pale green leaves cradle the full, ivory heads like a protective sun bonnet. In fact, the outer leaves are sometimes tied up around the head as it grows to keep the cauliflower creamy white. I like to simmer the florets in broth with potato and cilantro, then puree the mixture to make a delicate soup. To make a meal of it, add a salad of spring greens or Escarole Salad with Avocado and Oranges (page 50) and some crusty bread.

2 TABLESPOONS OLIVE OIL
1 LARGE ONION, THINLY SLICED
2 CLOVES GARLIC, MINCED
¼ CUP CHOPPED CILANTRO
1 POUND CAULIFLOWER FLORETS
1 BAKING POTATO (8 TO 10 OUNCES), PEELED, IN ½-INCH CUBES
2 CUPS HOMEMADE OR CANNED LOW-SODIUM CHICKEN BROTH
SALT AND FRESHLY GROUND BLACK PEPPER
1 CUP MILK

SERVES 6

Heat olive oil in a large pot over moderate heat. Add onion and saute until soft and sweet, about 10 minutes. Add garlic and cilantro and saute 1 minute to release garlic fragrance.

Add cauliflower, potato, broth, 3 cups water and salt and pepper to taste. Bring to a boil, then cover, adjust heat to maintain a bare simmer and cook until vegetables are tender, about 30 minutes.

Puree in a food processor or pass through a food mill. Return to a clean pot and stir in milk. Reheat to serving temperature. Taste and adjust seasoning.

sweet pea and green garlic soup

A few growers are starting to bring green garlic to the farmers' market, having experienced some demand from cooks. Harvested in spring, when it resembles a scallion and has yet to form a bulb, green garlic has a delicate flavor that is easily overpowered. To appreciate its character, you have to use a lot of it and take care not to mask it with other strong tastes. In this beautiful pea soup, inspired by a recipe in Carol Field's *The Italian Baker*, green garlic is a subtle but essential presence.

¼ CUP OLIVE OIL

3 CUPS THINLY SLICED GREEN GAR-LIC, WHITE AND PALE GREEN PARTS ONLY

3 CUPS SHELLED ENGLISH PEAS (FROM ABOUT 3 POUNDS UNSHELLED PEAS)

4 CUPS HOMEMADE OR CANNED LOW-SODIUM CHICKEN BROTH, OR MORE AS NEEDED

SALT AND FRESHLY GROUND BLACK PEPPER

8 SLICES DAY-OLD BAGUETTE

1 GARLIC CLOVE, HALVED

EXTRA VIRGIN OLIVE OIL FOR DRIZZLING

SERVES 4

Heat olive oil in a large pot over moderately low heat. Add garlic and saute 5 minutes, then cover and steam, stirring occasionally, until garlic is soft, about 5 more minutes. Add peas and 2½ cups broth. Bring to a simmer, adjust heat to maintain a gentle simmer and cook, uncovered, until peas are just tender, 5 to 10 minutes.

In a food processor or blender, puree half the soup until smooth. Return to the same pot and add enough broth to bring mixture to the consistency you like. Season with salt and pepper and reheat gently.

Toast the baguette slices until lightly colored. Rub on one side with a cut side of garlic. Drizzle with extra virgin olive oil.

Serve soup in warm bowls, topping each portion with a couple of toasts.

43

roasted beets with fennel oil

Fennel seed's licoricelike flavor complements the candy-sweet young beets you can find at the farmers' market in late spring and early summer. To capture the flavor, I crush the seeds in a mortar, then heat them gently in olive oil just until they impart their fragrance. The strained oil makes the beets glisten, and the subtle fennel flavor is captivating. For a particularly beautiful salad, try to buy small red and golden beets. Their tops will probably still be attached; if they are perky, you know the beets were just pulled. Save the greens, steam them, and dress them with olive oil and lemon.

¾ TEASPOON FENNEL SEEDS, CRUSHED IN A MORTAR OR SPICE GRINDER

2 TABLESPOONS EXTRA VIRGIN OLIVE OIL

1½ POUNDS SMALL BEETS, PREFERABLY A MIX OF RED AND GOLDEN (SEE NOTE)

1 TABLESPOON SHERRY VINEGAR

SALT

1 TABLESPOON THINLY SLICED FRESH CHIVES, OPTIONAL

SERVES 4

NOTE: If using both red and golden beets, bake them separately or the red beets will stain the golden ones. Dress them in separate bowls, using half the oil and vinegar for each. Serve them alongside each other, in separate mounds.

Heat fennel seeds and olive oil in a small skillet over low heat until oil is fragrant with fennel, about 5 minutes. Cool, then strain through a sieve.

Preheat oven to 375 degrees F. If greens are attached, remove all but ½ inch of the stems (so as not to pierce the beets) and reserve for another use. Put beets in a baking dish and add ¼ cup water. Cover tightly with a lid or aluminum foil and bake until a knife slips in easily, 40 to 45 minutes.

Cool slightly, then peel. Cut into quarters or, if very small, in half. Toss with strained oil and sherry vinegar. Season with salt. Transfer to a serving bowl or platter and top, if desired, with chives.

warm frisée and fava bean salad

A type of chicory with fine, frilly leaves and a blanched heart, frisée has a gentle bitterness that complements sweet fava beans. Look for a small head of frisée with a lot of white or pale yellow heart, and tear the leaves into small pieces so they're easy to eat.

2 POUNDS FAVA BEANS

2 OUNCES PANCETTA (1 SLICE, ¼ INCH THICK), SLICED CROSSWISE IN ¼ INCH PIECES

1 TABLESPOON EXTRA VIRGIN OLIVE OIL

2 SHALLOTS, MINCED

¼ POUND YOUNG, TENDER FRISÉE TORN INTO VERY SMALL PIECES

2 TABLESPOONS MINCED ITALIAN PARSLEY

1 TABLESPOON SHERRY VINEGAR

SALT AND FRESHLY GROUND BLACK PEPPER

SERVES 4

To double-peel fava beans: Shell the beans. Bring a large pot of water to a boil over high heat. Add beans and boil 2 minutes if large, 1 minute if small; drain and transfer to a bowl of ice water. Drain when cool, then remove the outer skin from each bean by pinching open the end of the bean opposite the end that connected it to the pod. The peeled bean will slip out easily. You should have about 1 to 1¼ cups peeled beans.

Saute pancetta in olive oil in a skillet over moderately low heat until it renders most of its fat and begins to crisp, about 5 minutes. Add shallots and sauté until softened, about 1 minute.

Put frisée in a serving bowl. Add contents of skillet, parsley and vinegar. Toss well, then add favas, season with salt and pepper and toss again. Taste and adjust seasoning.

peas with spring onions, prosciutto and parsley

In Northern California, spring onions—bulbing onions pulled before the bulb forms—show up in farmers' markets in step with the first peas, another example of nature's good timing. A generous amount of the mild spring onions, chopped and stirred in at the last minute, gives a bowl of sweet peas and prosciutto a gentle onion taste. I like peas so much I'll serve them as a separate first course, but you could serve these with lamb chops, veal scaloppine, baked salmon or an Easter ham.

3 TABLESPOONS EXTRA VIRGIN OLIVE OIL

1 LARGE CLOVE GARLIC, MINCED

4 CUPS SHELLED ENGLISH PEAS (FROM ABOUT 4 POUNDS UNSHELLED PEAS)

2 OUNCES PROSCIUTTO DI PARMA, MINCED

1 TABLESPOON CHOPPED ITALIAN PARSLEY

1 ½ CUPS CHOPPED SPRING ONIONS OR GREEN ONIONS (SCALLIONS), WHITE AND PALE GREEN PARTS ONLY

SALT AND FRESHLY GROUND BLACK PEPPER

Heat 2 tablespoons olive oil in a large skillet over moderate heat. Add garlic and saute 1 minute to release its fragrance. Add peas and prosciutto and stir to coat with seasonings. Add ¼ cup water, bring to a simmer, then cover and adjust heat to maintain a gentle simmer. Cook until peas are just tender, about 5 minutes.

Stir in parsley and spring or green onions and cook about 1 minute to wilt the onions slightly. Season to taste with salt and pepper. Just before serving, stir in remaining tablespoon olive oil.

SERVES 4

creamed feta with radishes, spring onions, mint and olives

I love the Persian way of beginning a meal: a platter of crisp green onions and radishes, feta cheese, pita bread and fresh herbs. You are meant to wrap a piece of cheese up in pita with a few leaves of mint, basil or dill and perhaps a length of green onion to make a little "sandwich." When spring onions (see page 76) and radishes turn up at my market, I like to make a variation of this Persian hors d'oeuvre, using feta cheese whipped with olive oil until it is smooth and spreadable. The exact components of the hors d'oeuvre can vary with what you find at the farmers' market, but to contrast with the creamy feta, there should be some crunchy element, such as neatly trimmed spring onions, radishes, pale hearts of romaine or sliced fennel. The herbs—mint, basil, dill, tarragon, cilantro or arugula—should be left in sprigs or whole leaves. I prefer the mild French sheep's milk feta for this recipe, but any other imported feta will work.

½ POUND FRENCH, GREEK OR BULGARIAN FETA CHEESE

1½ TABLESPOONS EXTRA VIRGIN OLIVE OIL

½ SMALL CLOVE GARLIC, THINLY SLICED

1 BUNCH RADISHES, TRIMMED

1 DOZEN SPRING ONIONS OR GREEN ONIONS (SCALLIONS), WHITE AND PALE GREEN PARTS ONLY

2 DOZEN KALAMATA OLIVES

HEARTS OF ROMAINE LETTUCE

FRESH MINT, BASIL OR DILL LEAVES

PITA BREAD

SERVES 4

Put the feta in a food processor with olive oil and garlic and blend until smooth and creamy. Transfer to a serving bowl or plate or spoon onto the middle of a large platter and surround with all the remaining ingredients.

escarole salad with avocado and oranges

At the farmers' market, look for escarole that has a large pale blanched heart. That's the choice part, crisp and mild. The outer, darker leaves can be tough and strong.

FOR THE VINAIGRETTE:

1 LARGE SHALLOT, MINCED

1 TABLESPOON CHAMPAGNE VIN-EGAR, OR MORE TO TASTE

3 TABLESPOONS EXTRA VIRGIN OLIVE OIL

SALT AND FRESHLY GROUND BLACK PEPPER

1 HEAD ESCAROLE

2 NAVEL ORANGES

1 RIPE BUT FIRM AVOCADO

2 TABLESPOONS CHOPPED ITALIAN PARSLEY

SERVES 4

To make the vinaigrette: In a small bowl, combine shallot, 1 table-spoon vinegar and the olive oil and whisk well. Season with salt and pepper. Taste and add more vinegar, if desired.

Clean escarole, discarding any battered outer pieces. Wash and drain leaves, tear into bite-sized pieces and dry thoroughly.

Cut a slice off both ends of 1 orange so it will stand upright. Stand orange on a cutting surface and, using a sharp knife, remove all the peel and white pith by slicing from top to bottom all the way around the orange, following the contour of the fruit. With the knife, cut along both sides of each orange segment to free the segment from its membrane. Put orange segments in a small bowl. Repeat with second orange.

Halve and pit the avocado. Use a soup spoon to remove each half from its shell in one piece. Lay cut side down and slice crosswise into ¼-inch-thick slices. Transfer avocado to a small bowl, season with salt and toss with enough of the vinaigrette to coat slices lightly.

Toss escarole with remaining vinaigrette and 1½ tablespoons parsley. Taste and adjust seasoning. Transfer to a serving bowl, interspersing layers of escarole with some of the avocados and oranges. Arrange the last of the avocados and oranges on top and sprinkle with remaining ½ tablespoon parsley.

catalan spinach

I can't visit Timo's, a funky San Francisco tapas bar, without having an order of chef Carlos Corredor's marvelous spinach. The following recipe is my attempt to re-create the taste of his, and I believe I have come pretty close. Enjoy it as a tapa with a chunk of bread and a glass of sherry, or as an accompaniment to calves' liver, rabbit, duck or pork. I also think it would be a delicious base for sauteed foie gras. At the farmers' market, look for tender spinach with thin stems.

1 TABLESPOON DRIED CURRANTS

2 TABLESPOONS PINE NUTS

2 BUNCHES FRESH SPINACH, ABOUT 14 OUNCES EACH

3 TABLESPOONS EXTRA VIRGIN OLIVE OIL

1 LARGE CLOVE GARLIC, MINCED

3 DRIED APRICOTS, IN 1/8-INCH DICE

SALT AND FRESHLY GROUND BLACK PEPPER

SERVES 4 AS A SMALL SIDE DISH

Place currants in a small bowl with warm water to cover and let stand 30 minutes to soften, then drain.

Preheat oven to 325 degrees F. Toast pine nuts on a baking sheet until they are golden brown and fragrant, 12 to 15 minutes.

Wash spinach well in a sink filled with cold water. Remove and discard thick stems, and drain leaves in a colander. Repeat washing if necessary to remove all grit and drain again. Place spinach in a large pot with just the water clinging to the leaves. Cover and cook over moderate heat, stirring occasionally, until leaves are just wilted, 3 to 5 minutes. Drain in a sieve under cold running water. Squeeze between your hands to remove excess moisture.

Heat olive oil in a 10-inch skillet over moderate heat. Add garlic and saute until it colors slightly, about 2 minutes. Add spinach, tossing to separate the leaves and coat them with oil. Add currants, pine nuts and dried apricots. Toss to distribute evenly. Season with salt and pepper. Cook, stirring occasionally, until spinach is hot throughout, 2 to 3 minutes. Serve immediately.

cornmeal cake with strawberries

Its tender, golden crumb makes this cake a good foundation for a sort of unstructured strawberry shortcake. Serve it in wedges with a puddle of juicy crushed berries and soft whipped cream. In summer, enjoy it with blackberries, raspberries, peaches or a combination of ripe fruits from the farmers' market. It wouldn't hurt to flavor the whipped cream with a little rum or brandy.

FOR THE CAKE:

UNSALTED BUTTER AND CORNMEAL FOR PREPARING THE PAN

1¼ CUPS SIFTED CAKE FLOUR

6 TABLESPOONS YELLOW CORNMEAL

2 TEASPOONS BAKING POWDER

¼ TEASPOON SALT

½ CUP UNSALTED BUTTER, AT ROOM TEMPERATURE

1 CUP SUGAR

2 LARGE EGGS

1 TEASPOON GRATED LEMON ZEST

½ CUP MILK

1 TEASPOON VANILLA EXTRACT

2 BASKETS (1 PINT EACH) STRAWBERRIES

SUGAR TO TASTE, PLUS 2 TEASPOONS

FRESH LEMON JUICE

1 CUP HEAVY CREAM

MAKES ONE 9-INCH CAKE, TO SERVE 8

53

To make the cake: Preheat oven to 350 degrees F. Butter the bottom and sides of a 9-inch round cake pan with 2-inch sides. Line the bottom with wax paper and butter the paper. Dust the pan bottom and sides with cornmeal, shaking out excess.

In a bowl, stir together the cake flour, cornmeal, baking powder and salt.

In an electric mixer, beat butter until creamy. Add sugar gradually and beat, scraping down sides of bowl once or twice, until creamy and light. Add eggs one at a time, beating well after each addition. Add lemon zest.

Combine milk and vanilla extract. With mixer on low speed, add dry ingredients in three batches, alternating with milk. Beat just until blended, scraping down sides of bowl once or twice. Spread batter evenly in prepared pan.

Bake until top is golden brown and firm to the touch, 35 to 40 minutes. Let cool in pan 20 minutes. Invert the cake onto a rack, then reinvert onto another rack. Cool to room temperature, then transfer to a serving platter.

Hull the strawberries. Put half of them in a large bowl and crush with a potato masher. Slice the remaining strawberries and add to the bowl. Sweeten to taste with sugar. Add enough lemon juice to give the mixture a refreshing tart edge. Cover and chill.

Just before serving, whip cream to soft peaks with 2 teaspoons sugar.

Cut the cake into 8 portions and transfer to serving plates. Divide the berries and the cream evenly among the portions.

spinach salad with roasted beets and feta

Some farmers are now bringing the most tender baby spinach to the market, already washed and dried and ready to use in salads. It is a great convenience that has probably done more than any cartoon character ever did to get people to eat this nutritious vegetable. One enthusiastic grower told me that he met his wife through baby spinach. (He left me to imagine the details.) I make no claims for the matchmaking power of baby spinach, but I do know that it marries well with beets.

1 POUND SMALL BEETS

4 TEASPOONS SHERRY VINEGAR, PLUS MORE AS NEEDED

2 CLOVES GARLIC, FINELY MINCED

¼ CUP EXTRA VIRGIN OLIVE OIL

SALT AND FRESHLY GROUND BLACK PEPPER

¼ RED ONION, THINLY SLICED

½ POUND BABY SPINACH LEAVES

3 OUNCES GREEK, BULGARIAN OR FRENCH FETA CHEESE

SERVES 4

Preheat oven to 375 degrees F. If beet greens are attached, remove all but ½ inch of the stems (so as not to pierce the beets) and reserve for another use. Put beets in a baking dish with ¼ cup water. Cover tightly and bake until a small knife slips in easily, 40 to 45 minutes. Cool slightly, then peel. Let cool completely, then cut into ½ inch wedges.

In a small bowl, whisk together 4 teaspoons vinegar, the garlic, the olive oil, and salt and pepper to taste.

In a small bowl, toss together beets and red onion with about half of the dressing. Let stand 10 minutes to absorb flavors, then taste and sprinkle with a little more vinegar if necessary.

In a large bowl, toss spinach with remaining dressing. Taste and adjust seasoning. Divide equally among 4 plates. Top with beets and onions, again dividing equally. Crumble feta evenly over each salad.

tapioca pudding with strawberry-rhubarb sauce

Strawberries and rhubarb have a natural affinity that cooks have long exploited in pies and crisps. This homespun dessert is another possibility for those times when you find the two crops at the farmers' market together. I like to serve it in a balloon wineglass so you can see the garnet red sauce underneath the pudding. You will have a lot of sauce left over, but you will be glad for it. Serve it over toast, biscuits, strawberry shortcake, angel food cake, Cornmeal Cake with Strawberries (page 53), pancakes or ice cream, or stir it into yogurt. It will keep, refrigerated, for at least a week. You can also halve the sauce recipe successfully.

FOR THE PUDDING:

¼ CUP QUICK-COOKING TAPIOCA
6 TABLESPOONS SUGAR
3 CUPS MILK
2 EGGS, WELL BEATEN
1 TEASPOON VANILLA EXTRACT

FOR THE SAUCE:

1 BASKET (1 PINT) STRAWBERRIES
½ POUND RHUBARB, IN ½-INCH WIDTHS
6 TO 8 TABLESPOONS SUGAR
2 TABLESPOONS FRESH ORANGE JUICE

SERVES 6

To make the pudding: Combine tapioca, sugar, milk and eggs in a saucepan. Let stand 5 minutes. Cook over moderate heat, stirring constantly, until mixture comes to a rolling boil. Immediately remove from heat, transfer to a bowl and stir in vanilla extract. Let cool without stirring, then cover and chill. Pudding will thicken as it cools.

To make the sauce: Hull and quarter strawberries. In a saucepan, combine strawberries, rhubarb, 6 tablespoons sugar and orange juice. Bring to a simmer over moderate heat, stirring to dissolve sugar. Cover, adjust heat to maintain a gentle simmer and cook until fruit softens and forms a sauce, about 10 minutes. Watch carefully to make sure mixture doesn't boil up and spill over the pan. Uncover, stir well, then taste. Add up to 2 tablespoons more sugar if necessary, then transfer to a bowl to cool. Cover and refrigerate until cold.

To serve, put a generous tablespoon of strawberry-rhubarb sauce in each of 6 balloon wineglasses or compote dishes. Top with ½ cup tapioca.

three bistro salads

As I discovered in the months I spent in Paris after college, being nearly penniless in that city is no impediment to eating well. I soon found a collection of likeable working-class bistros whose daily menus fell within my budget. Invariably, the first course was a selection of simple vegetable salads in white bowls. Some were raw, like grated carrots with olive oil, thinly sliced fennel in vinaigrette or creamy celery root rémoulade. Some were cooked, such as grated beets with garlic or vinegary potato salad with shallots and parsley.

In spring, I like to re-create these bistro salads with market vegetables, seving them with a bowl of Niçoise olives, a French baguette, and occasionally, some sliced pâté.

GRATED BEET SALAD:

¾ POUND BEETS (3 MEDIUM OR 2 LARGE)

1 TABLESPOON EXTRA VIRGIN OLIVE OIL

2 TEASPOONS RED WINE VINEGAR

1 SMALL CLOVE GARLIC, FINELY MINCED

SALT

GRATED CARROT SALAD:

½ POUND CARROTS

1½ TABLESPOONS EXTRA VIRGIN OLIVE OIL

1 TABLESPOON FRESH LEMON JUICE

1 SMALL CLOVE GARLIC, FINELY MINCED

2 TEASPOONS CHOPPED FRESH CHIVES

SALT

MARINATED FENNEL SALAD:

2 TABLESPOONS EXTRA VIRGIN OLIVE OIL

1 TABLESPOON FRESH LEMON JUICE

1 SHALLOT, MINCED

½ TABLESPOON MINCED ITALIAN PARSLEY

SALT AND FRESHLY GROUND BLACK PEPPER

1 LARGE OR 2 SMALL FENNEL BULBS

SERVES 4

Grated Beet Salad: Preheat oven to 375 degrees F. If beet greens are attached, remove all but ½ inch of the stems (so as not to pierce the beets) and reserve for another use. Put beets in a baking dish with ¼ cup water. Cover and bake until a small knife slips in easily—about 50 minutes for medium beets. Cool slightly, then peel. Let cool completely. Grate the beets on the large-holed side of a four-sided grater. Transfer to a bowl. Stir in olive oil, wine vinegar, garlic and salt to taste. Taste and adjust seasoning.

Grated Carrot Salad: Peel carrots; grate on the large-holed side of a four-sided grater. Transfer to a bowl and stir in olive oil, lemon juice, garlic, chives and salt to taste. Taste and adjust seasoning.

Marinated Fennel Salad: In a medium bowl, combine olive oil, lemon juice, shallot, parsley, and salt and pepper to taste. Whisk to blend.

Remove fennel stalks, if attached. Halve fennel bulb(s) lengthwise. Cut away core. If outer layer of bulb half seems tough or fibrous, remove it. Lay each half cut side down and slice crosswise as thinly as possible. Transfer sliced fennel to bowl with dressing and toss to coat. Taste and adjust seasoning. Let stand 30 minutes before serving.

turnip and turnip greens soup

At my local supermarket, the turnips are always neatly scrubbed, trimmed and displayed, but the corresponding turnip greens are nowhere to be found. I suspect they are removed, either by the packer or by the store, because they have passed their prime. At the farmers' market, you are more likely to find turnips with greens attached. The sprightly tops are your guarantee that the roots were recently harvested. Besides their role as a freshness indicator, the greens make a nutritious soup when pureed with the cooked roots and a little rice for body. This recipe was inspired by one from Chez Panisse—the famed Berkeley, California, restaurant—that appeared in *Food & Wine* magazine.

2 TABLESPOONS UNSALTED BUTTER, PLUS MORE FOR GARNISH

1 YELLOW ONION, FINELY CHOPPED

2 CLOVES GARLIC, MINCED

1½ POUNDS TURNIPS, PEELED AND DICED

½ CUP ARBORIO RICE

SALT AND FRESHLY GROUND BLACK PEPPER

6 CUPS HOMEMADE CHICKEN BROTH, OR 3 CUPS CANNED LOW-SODIUM BROTH MIXED WITH 3 CUPS WATER

½ POUND TURNIP GREEN LEAVES (NO STEMS), SLICED INTO RIBBONS

1½ TABLESPOONS CHOPPED FRESH DILL

SERVES 6

Melt 2 tablespoons butter in a large pot over moderately low heat. Add onion and saute until soft, about 10 minutes. Add garlic and saute 1 minute to release its fragrance. Add turnips and rice, season with salt and pepper and stir to coat with seasonings. Add 3 cups broth, bring to a simmer, then cover and adjust heat to maintain a gentle simmer. Cook 15 minutes.

Stir in turnip greens, cover and simmer until turnips, greens and rice are soft, about 5 more minutes. Stir in dill. Transfer to a food processor or blender, in batches if necessary, and blend until smooth. Return to pot and stir in remaining broth to achieve a souplike consistency. Taste and adjust seasoning.

Reheat and serve in warm bowls, garnishing each portion with a thin sliver of butter.

spanish tortilla with spring vegetables

Every tapas bar in Spain has a thick, round tortilla on the counter, waiting for customers to order a slice with a glass of sherry. These open-faced omelets give the cook free rein to use whatever vegetables were best at the market or whatever bits of ham, sausage or greens might be on hand. It is a recipe worth mastering because it easily adapts to any season and to what the market provides. In winter, you might replace the peas and fava beans with mushrooms; in summer, you can fashion a tortilla with zucchini and roasted red peppers.

I like my tortillas thick with sliced potatoes and vegetables, with just enough egg to bind the layers. Turned out onto a serving platter or cutting board, the golden round announces the sherry hour. Just don't cut into it too soon; it needs to rest.

5 TABLESPOONS EXTRA VIRGIN OLIVE OIL, PLUS UP TO 1 ADDITIONAL TABLESPOON

1½ POUNDS BAKING POTATOES, PEELED AND SLICED ⅛ INCH THICK

SALT AND FRESHLY GROUND BLACK PEPPER

3 CUPS THINLY SLICED LEEKS, WHITE AND PALE GREEN PARTS ONLY

6 LARGE EGGS, LIGHTLY BEATEN

½ CUP COOKED ENGLISH PEAS (ABOUT ½ POUND UNSHELLED PEAS)

½ CUP PEELED FAVA BEANS (ABOUT 1 POUND UNSHELLED FAVA BEANS; SEE PAGE 46)

SERVES 4 AS A LUNCH DISH, 6 AS AN APPETIZER

Heat 4 tablespoons olive oil in a 12- to 14-inch nonstick skillet over high heat. Add potatoes, season highly with salt and pepper and saute, tossing often, until tender, about 10 minutes. Drain potatoes in a sieve set over a bowl. Let cool. (If you have only a smaller nonstick skillet, fry the potatoes in two batches, using 2 tablespoons oil each time.)

Return skillet to moderate heat and add 1 tablespoon olive oil. When hot, add leeks, season with salt and pepper and toss to coat with seasonings. Cover, reduce heat to moderately low and cook until leeks are tender, about 15 minutes. Let cool.

In a large bowl, combine eggs, potatoes, leeks, peas and fava beans. Season with salt and pepper, stir well, then let stand for 10 minutes.

Measure oil drained from potatoes, if any. Add enough olive oil to make 1 tablespoon. Heat a 10-inch skillet over high heat. When hot, add oil. When oil is hot, add egg mixture, spreading it into an even layer. It will bubble vigorously around the edges. Immediately lower heat to moderately low and cook 10 to 12 minutes. The omelet will still be underdone on the surface. Invert a cookie sheet over the skillet. Grasping the skillet handle with one hand and holding the cookie sheet in place with the other, flip the skillet so the tortilla falls onto the cookie sheet. Immediately slide it back into the skillet, cooked side up. (Some moist bits of egg may stick to the cookie sheet; that's okay.) Cook an additional 10 to 12 minutes, then invert onto a serving platter. Let stand at least 20 minutes before serving.

THE MARKET IN

summer

Peach juice dripping down a chin. Nectar oozing from a fig. Corn spilling from a truck. The summer farmers' market puts nature's exuberance on display, in booth after booth of seductive produce. When I walk the market, I feel like a child at an amusement park, drawn this way by the perfume of nectarines, that way by vine-ripe tomatoes. The chief challenge is restricting myself to what my household can eat.

One thing I love about the summer market is how easily my purchases come together into appealing dishes. Slender green beans and halved cherry tomatoes make one simple salad. Crisp cucumbers, red onions and arugula combine for another; tomatoes, corn and basil for a third. These are the sort of impromptu inventions that happen when I get home and see what I've bought. I could, with equal success, have paired the green beans with corn and arugula, the cucumbers with cherry tomatoes and basil. Sometimes a summer dinner at my house is nothing but vegetables with aioli—thick, fresh garlic mayonnaise with a platter of ripe tomatoes and steamed baby green beans, potatoes and summer squash.

Summer fruits harmonize just as naturally. Figs, nectarines and berries make a beautiful compote in a wine syrup flavored with lemon verbena or scented geraniums. White peaches can be sliced and floated in a syrup tinted with raspberry puree. If you master a flaky pie crust, you can make glistening fruit galettes with whatever summer fruit is best: figs, raspberries, peaches, nectarines or a combination.

Many small growers have to recoup most of their year-long investment during a few brief weeks in summer. With their purchases, farmers' market shoppers have the pleasure of rewarding the farmer directly.

berries

Picked dead-ripe and brought to a farmers' market the next day, John Lagier's blackberries are snapped up quickly. One extra day on the plant makes all the difference in sugar accumulation, says Lagier, but ripeness brings fragility. Fortunately, he can pamper his berries on the short trip from his Escalon, California, field to market; growers who ship to distributors or supermarkets must pick their berries on the green side.

You may find a variety of blackberries at a summer farmers' market: boysenberries, marionberries, loganberries and olallieberries are all blackberry hybrids, with subtly different tastes and textures. In addition to the familiar red raspberries, keep an eye out for golden or black ones, equally as fragrant and flavorful. And the farmers' market is your best bet for finding small blueberries, which tend to have better flavor—but less eye appeal—than the large ones.

selection: "You can tell a ripe blackberry by its sheen," says Lagier. It should have a rich, dark color and pleasing aroma. Large berries tend to be tastier than small ones. The drupelets —the little sacs that make up the berry—should be big and plump, indicating that the fruit wasn't stressed and had time to mature. Raspberries, too, should have full drupelets and a seductive perfume. With blueberries, which don't have much aroma, look for solid dark blue color—no reddish green spots—and for a powdery bloom, which indicates a berry that was recently picked and not overhandled. Blueberry flavor is all in the skin, says Lagier, which is why the tiny wild blueberries taste so good. For all berries, check the underside of the container to make sure it isn't splotched with the juice of crushed berries.

storage: Ripe berries don't store well. Keep them refrigerated and dry, perhaps with a paper towel in the container to collect any moisture. So that fragile berries don't crush one another, you may want to arrange them in a single layer on a paper towel–lined tray, then cover with plastic and refrigerate.

corn

To find the most succulent corn at the farmers' market, look for a sign that says "Picked Today." Even though many farmers are growing new strains of corn that have been bred to stay sweet longer, freshness still counts. Corn loses moisture once harvested, and its sugar does convert to starch, albeit more slowly in genetically altered varieties.

Harder than finding sweet corn these days is finding corn that isn't too sweet. Some new "supersweet" varieties contain twice as much sugar as old-fashioned corn and hold onto it longer. The result, sometimes, is an ear of corn that tastes more like candy than like a vegetable. I look instead for old-fashioned standards such as Golden Bantam and

Country Gentleman, or for sugar-enhanced varieties, including Silver Queen or Platinum Lady. Sugar-enhanced corn has also been genetically modified to enhance sweetness and tenderness, but these varieties do not sacrifice the corn flavor.

Corn farmers are always proud of their harvest, and it's a pleasure to hear their boasts first-hand—an experience that only a farmers' market can provide.

selection: Look for well-filled-out ears with a moist, pale stem end and a fresh-looking tassel (the silky strings at the tip). The tip should not be brown or mushy, and the kernels under the husk should be plump and milky. White varieties tend to be sweeter and more tender, yellow varieties to have a fuller corn flavor.

storage: Take corn home immediately; don't let it sit in a hot trunk. Refrigerate it in a plastic bag unhusked and cook it as soon as possible.

cucumbers

The common supermarket cucumber, plump and waxy and filled with tough seeds, bears little resemblance to the flavorful cucumbers found at farmers' market these days. "In my mind, they're not even cucumbers," says Nick Atallah of the tough-skinned variety favored by most large-scale commercial growers. Pumped up with water to make them grow fast, then waxed to keep the moisture in, these cucumbers have none of the appeal of the small, thin-skinned Mediterranean cucumbers that Atallah recalls from his Lebanese childhood.

Today he is growing those remembered cucumbers in a Northern California greenhouse and taking them to farmers' markets within a day or two of harvest. You may not find Atallah's Mediterranean cucumbers at your farmers' market, but you will probably discover other types that have the commercial cucumber beat hands-down: long, slender Japanese cucumbers; round, yellow lemon cucumbers; or pale green, ridged Armenian cucumbers. When just harvested, these varieties are so crisp and tasty that you will want to eat them out of hand as a refreshing summer snack.

selection: Cucumbers should be firm and turgid. If they are at all limp or shriveled, they are losing moisture and weren't just picked. Ask for samples at the market to find which varieties you like best. The lemon cucumber is named for its appearance, not for its flavor, which is sweet and mild. Unless very young, they may need peeling. Japanese cucumbers never do; I love their crisp, juicy taste and often will cut them into long fingers for a snack. The ridged Armenian cucumbers make particularly pretty slices for salads.

storage: Cucumbers simply don't store well. Buy what you can eat within two or three days. Atallah stores his cucumbers in a plastic-lidded container, with a paper towel on the bottom and top and a paper towel between layers.

eggplants

If you want to experience eggplant in all its variety, shop at a farmers' market. Interest in heirloom varieties and in bringing to market what others don't have has prompted farmers' market growers to peruse seed catalogs for something different.

Look for Rosa Bianca eggplant, the favorite of California grower Paul Holmes and many others. This stunningly beautiful fruit has ivory skin with lavender markings and a creamy flesh devoid of bitterness. Or take home a few Asian Brides, a long, slender Japanese variety in a white robe streaked with lavender. They, too, have none of the bitterness that turns some people off of globe eggplants. Sample the White Egg variety, whose earlier relatives clearly inspired the vegetable's English name. And if you patronize a farmers' market that serves an Asian clientele, you may find cherry-sized green eggplants for pickling or adding to curries.

The long, slender eggplants tend to have more compact, less watery flesh; fewer seeds; more delicate skins and a milder flavor with no bitterness. I prefer them for most uses, although there are times when only a big, thick slice from a globe eggplant will do.

selection: A shiny eggplant is probably a fresh eggplant. When growers harvest, they look for that gloss, as well as full color and a texture that gives slightly to pressure. A soft eggplant is either overmature or has been off the plant for a long time and lost moisture. The skin should be taut, not withered. A given variety can mature eggplants in a range of sizes, but in general, a larger eggplant is an older eggplant, more likely to be pithy, seedy or soft.

storage: If you are going to use your eggplant within a day or two, store at cool room temperature. For longer storage, store in a loose plastic bag in the refrigerator crisper.

figs

"We've been trained that anything that's ugly is no good," says grower Rick Knoll, "but that's the wrong way of looking at figs. They have to be gushy, ugly and soft before they're good."

The vast majority of figs are picked too early, claims Knoll. They need to ripen on the tree, because they won't ripen off of it. Unfortunately, few supermarkets are willing to give a soft, ripe fig the pampered handling it needs. But growers who attend farmers' markets can pick their figs dead-ripe and count on finding customers who don't care that the fruit's not picture-perfect.

People who complain about the cost of figs have never harvested them, says the grower. Figs are brutal on workers' hands because the stem "bleeds" latex when it's cut. The latex so irritates the cuticles and the area under the nails that pickers have to tape their fingers like football players do. At night, workers soak their hands with medicinal herbs Knoll gives them; even so, he has to maintain two crews so no one picks too many days in a row.

selection: A ripe fig is a soft fig. The Kadota should have a drop of "honey" at the end; Black Missions taste best when they start to shrivel. Avoid figs with any sign of mold.

storage: Don't store figs in plastic; they don't like the humidity. Refrigerate them in a paper bag or, better yet, on a plate. They should keep for a week.

garlic

Planted from individual cloves in the fall, garlic overwinters in California, putting up its green, aromatic shoots in early spring (see page 27). In April and May, the bulb swells and divides into more new cloves, each separated from the other by a thin skin. By early summer it is ready to harvest.

After harvest, the bulbs—with greens attached—are left to dry in the field for a few days, then they are bundled and dried for another week or so indoors. Typically, before taking them to market, the grower cuts off the greens and peels off any dirty outer papery skin so the garlic bulb looks clean and white. Some farmers' market growers leave the greens attached and use them to braid several bulbs into long ropes.

Dru Rivers of Northern California's Full Belly Farm always takes some garlic to the farmers' market in its fresh-dug (uncured) state. "I think that's when its flavor is best," says Rivers. "We think of garlic as a storage crop, but it's the same as any produce. As soon as it's picked, it's best."

selection: Go ahead, squeeze the garlic. The bulb should feel firm and plump. I look for bulbs that have largish cloves because tiny ones are tedious to peel. You probably won't have problems with summer garlic, but if you are buying storage garlic later in the year, avoid any with signs of sooty mold or sprouting cloves.

storage: Keep garlic in a cool, dark, dry place—not next to or over the kitchen stove. "The garlic that keeps the best for me is braided and hung somewhere cool and dark," says Rivers. "Maybe it's because, when you cut off the greens, you leave open a spot where things can go bad."

green beans

If you want a fresh bean with a crisp snap, shop at farmers' markets. Most farmers pick one day and go to market the next, or at most two days later. That's important, because green beans quickly head downhill after harvest, losing their moisture and initial sweetness and becoming limp.

Many farmers' markets offer bean varieties you are unlikely to find at any but the best-stocked supermarkets—varieties like the flat Romano ("the best-tasting green bean grown by far," says California grower Denesse Willey), yellow wax or yellow Romano beans, or the superslender filet beans known in French as *haricots verts*.

Yard-long beans, popular among Asian customers at farmers' markets, are actually a climbing relative of southern peas, such as black-eyed peas and purple hull peas. The pods can be light green or dark green, purple, red, even black, says grower Alex Causey. And their name is not an exaggeration. Some varieties—not all—truly do produce three-foot-long pods.

selection: Snap beans should be crisp and have full, bright color. They also should feel a little fuzzy. "Here's a trick senior citizens taught me," says California grower Molly Gean. "If they stick to your clothes, they're fresh." Filet beans should be slender, less than ¼ inch thick in general. Any larger and they will probably be tough. Yard-long beans never have the crispness of a snap bean, but they should not feel limp.

storage: "I don't recommend that people store them," says Willey. "The whole idea behind getting the fresh beans is to eat them fresh." But if you must keep them a few days, Gean suggests putting them in a paper bag inside a plastic bag, then refrigerating in the crisper.

herbs

In many dishes, fresh herbs provide the interest that makes a diner want to keep on eating. A minestrone without parsley, basil, marjoram or oregano would taste flat and uninteresting. And just imagine the relative allure of two chickens, roasted with and without herbs.

At many farmers' markets, shoppers can purchase not only an array of potted herbs for their garden, but also a variety of fresh-cut herbs for their kitchen. And chances are these cut herbs are fresher—and, therefore, more aromatic—than what's available at the grocery store. The aromatic essence of an herb is volatile, says California grower Leonard Diggs; it dissipates quickly after harvest. He picks his herbs the afternoon before an early-morning farmers' market to guarantee customers a fragrant product with the longest-possible postmarket life.

For those who may not have a lot of familiarity with them, here are suggestions for using some of the more common fresh herbs:

BASIL The principal ingredient in pesto, basil enhances almost every summer and early autumn vegetable. Scatter leaves over a tomato salad or add to tomato sauce. Make a basil butter for corn on the cob. Pair with green bean salads or cooked okra, eggplant, zucchini or roasted peppers. For variety, experiment with the many scented and colored basils that growers are bringing to market now, such as lemon, anise, Thai, cinnamon and purple basils.

CHERVIL The subtle, licoricelike flavor of fresh chervil is at home in scrambled eggs, in potato salad, with green beans, cucumbers, spinach and tomatoes. Or add small sprigs to a green salad. It also complements mild-flavored fish. Add chopped shallots and chervil to a mayonnaise for poached salmon or sea bass.

CHIVES An onion relative, chives prove it with the delicate flavor they release when cut. Snip with scissors or slice thinly with a knife. Add to potato salad, egg salad, omelets or other egg dishes, steamed carrots, cauliflower, asparagus or beets, or sprinkle over fresh cottage or ricotta cheese. Chives also enhance fresh and smoked fish. Keep your eye out for garlic chives, which add a subtle, pleasant garlic note to dishes.

CILANTRO An essential culinary herb in Central and South America, China, Southeast Asia, North Africa and India, cilantro (also known as fresh coriander or Chinese parsley) has a growing fan club in this country. Add it to guacamole and salsa, black bean or pinto bean stews and soups, and corn preparations. Moroccan cooks stir the leaves into salads of roasted peppers and tomatoes. Chinese cooks add it to soups, steamed fish and stir-fries. Indians use it to season yogurt salads made with cucumber and tomato and braised vegetables such as eggplant, okra, potatoes or peas in tomato sauce.

DILL Chop feathery dill leaves and add to carrots, cauliflower, summer squashes, beets, brussels sprouts, cabbage, cucumbers, artichokes, spinach or leeks. Dill also enhances shrimp, salmon and lamb. To make proper dill pickles, you will need the flowering heads.

MARJORAM Add chopped marjoram to tomato sauce, green beans, artichokes or to a saute of sausage and peppers. Marjoram also enhances chicken and red meats.

MINT Use mint with artichokes, green beans, beets, carrots, cauliflower, cucumbers, eggplants, peas, summer squashes and hard-shelled squashes. Add chopped mint to a yogurt sauce for grilled lamb or to a shrimp salad. Flavor a poaching syrup with mint leaves before adding pears, peaches or other fruits.

OREGANO Add oregano to tomato sauce and to hearty preparations of green beans, summer squash, peppers and eggplant. Use it sparingly with vegetables, as it has an aggressive flavor. You can use it more liberally with chicken, rabbit or pork. It's also agreeable, in modest doses, with swordfish, tuna and shrimp.

PARSLEY The sprightly flavor of this ubiquitous herb freshens just about any vegetable preparation, apart from the cooking greens (chard, kale and collards, for example), whose own strong character would obscure it. Instead of putting a decorative sprig on the side of the plate, chop the parsley and add it at the last minute to vegetable dishes that need a lift.

A handful of chopped parsley also invigorates a green salad, especially one made with pale escarole, endive or hearts of butter lettuce. I prefer the flavor of flat-leaf parsley (often called Italian parsley), but curly parsley is a suitable substitute.

ROSEMARY Among the most pungent of herbs, rosemary should be used with restraint. Add a few sprigs to a pan of small potatoes before roasting, or leave a sprig in a tomato sauce or a pot of beans just long enough to imbue the dish with a subtle rosemary character. Rosemary flatters chicken, rabbit, turkey and virtually every red meat.

SAGE Tuck whole sage leaves around potatoes in a casserole before roasting, or add a little chopped sage to a tomato sauce or to sauteed mushrooms. Sage leaves crisped in butter make a delicious garnish for pumpkin ravioli or fettuccine with mushrooms. But in my kitchen, sage is primarily a meat herb. It enhances chicken livers and calves' liver, pork chops, turkey stuffing, veal scaloppine and braised breast of veal.

TARRAGON This herb's mild licorice flavor particularly complements spring vegetables. Add it to peas, asparagus, artichokes, leeks, beets, carrots and cauliflower. It also flatters green beans, potatoes, broccoli and mushrooms. Use it on delicate white fish or salmon, as well as with veal, pork or chicken. A sprig of tarragon slipped into a bottle of white wine vinegar will impart its character in just a few days; use the tarragon vinegar for salad dressings or for flavoring steamed cauliflower or roast beets.

THYME French cooks look to thyme to flavor potatoes, tomato sauce, eggplant, zucchini, peppers, hard-shelled squashes and tomato-based braises such as ratatouille. They also use it in meat cookery, with roast or grilled lamb, sauteed chicken or rabbit, and stews of beef or veal.

selection: Woody herbs such as rosemary and thyme hold up well after harvest and are likely to be in pretty good shape at the farmers' market. Nonwoody herbs decline more quickly, says Diggs, becoming limp or showing signs of decay. Choose specimens that look fresh and perky; limp herbs have lost moisture and probably can't be revived.

storage: Woody herbs can be refrigerated in a paper bag or left at room temperature, which will dry them out gradually. To air-dry for long keeping, tie sprigs in bunches with string and hang upside-down at room temperature. When fully dry, remove the leaves from the stems and store in airtight containers. Fresh herbs are more demanding and not good keepers in any case. Parsley and cilantro do well if refrigerated with the stem ends in a glass of water and a plastic bag over the top. Changing the water every couple of days will slow deterioration. Refrigerate other herbs wrapped in damp paper towels and placed inside a plastic bag. Basil in particular is hard to please in its postharvest life. You can wrap the bunch in damp newspaper and place inside a plastic bag, but this only buys you a little time. The best strategy is to use basil soon after purchase.

melons

Unlike supermarket shoppers, whose choices are usually limited to cantaloupe, Casaba, honeydew and watermelon, patrons at many farmers' markets will find the prized French Charentais, the Israeli Galia, or the white-meated Persian Kharboozeh Mashedi, the favorite of fifth-generation California melon grower Dave Fredericks. The latter can reach 15 percent sugar content, almost twice as sweet as a typical supermarket honeydew, says Fredericks.

Melons develop a lot of their sugar during the last few days on the vine. The aroma intensifies, the blossom end softens and, in some varieties, the surface becomes a little sticky or tacky. A grower who waits for that final spurt of vine ripening will probably deliver to customers a sweet, flavorful melon. But many growers who sell to supermarkets can't afford to wait. They pick their melons underripe so that the fruit can stand up to the rigors of shipping.

In grocery stores, you often see shoppers thumping melons, shaking them, sniffing them or turning in frustration to the produce manager for help in picking a good one. At the farmers' market, the challenge is easier because you can often taste before you buy. A farmers' market is a great place to learn about melons you might want to grow in your own garden and to taste exquisite varieties that, for various reasons, don't have mass-market potential.

selection: So how *do* you find a ripe one? The telltale signs vary depending on the melon type, so generalizations are difficult. Here are some guidelines, however: With netted melons like cantaloupes, the background color between the raised netting should be tan or gold, not greenish. Smooth-skinned honeydews should have a velvety, slightly sticky feel and be creamy yellow not greenish white. With most ripe netted and smooth-skinned melons (watermelons aside), the blossom end will be fragrant and give slightly to pressure. (Incidentally, Fredericks says that the blossom end of a melon is the sweetest; if you have a special guest, cut his or her portion from that end.) For all types but watermelons, if you shake it and hear seeds rattling, don't buy it, says Fredericks. The loose seeds indicate the melon is starting to break down. When a watermelon is ripe, its skin turns hard and dull and it often develops a yellow patch where it touched the ground. "Hold it like a baby and slap it on the bottom," advises Fredericks. "It should sound like you're hitting a jug of water. That's when you know you've really got a good one."

storage: If your melon feels hard, leave it at cool room temperature for a few days to soften slightly. (It's not really ripening—melons don't ripen off the vine—but its flesh will soften.) When the melon feels like it has the proper amount of "give," refrigerate it. So-called Christmas melons and Santa Claus melons are renowned for their longevity. You can keep them in a cool place for a couple of months and bring them out for Christmas.

nectarines

The California nectarines from Debbie Hurley's Summer Harvest Farms win converts because they are tree-ripened, picked five to seven days after most commercial growers would pick. The sugar content rises significantly during that crucial last week, but the fruit also becomes too soft to ship. Hurley tries to get her nectarines to a farmers' market within a day or two of harvest; in contrast, she says, it wouldn't be unusual for nectarines to take two to three weeks to reach an East Coast supermarket shelf.

Another difference between her fruit and typical grocery store nectarines is that her crew will pick each variety four to five times during its harvest period to get individual nectarines at peak ripeness. "If you were growing commercially," says Hurley, "the maximum you would do would be three picks of a variety, and usually not even that. Usually it's a single large pick, and then what's called a 'strip,'"—in other words, everything comes off, ready or not.

Hurley and her husband, John, grow some 25 nectarine varieties. When selecting new trees, they tell their suppliers that they don't care about shippability or color. "We tell them we want flavor and juice," says Hurley. "It's nice if they're beautiful, but they don't have to be because our customers are going to have the opportunity to taste before they buy."

selection: Look for fully colored, aromatic fruit with a bit of give to it, advises Hurley, although color can be deceptive. Some varieties naturally develop more color than others, but you should never settle for nectarines with any green tinge. In general, white nectarines such as Arctic Rose and Arctic Snow have more sugar and less acid than yellow varieties.

storage: Ideally, says Hurley, customers take her nectarines home, keep them in a cool, dry part of the kitchen and enjoy them within a few days. If you have bought more nectarines than you can eat quickly, keep some out and refrigerate the others, even if they are firm. Take them out of the refrigerator two to three days before you need them and let soften at room temperature.

okra

The okra I find in grocery stores is usually so beat-up, brown and sad looking that I'm not inspired to cook it. But the farmers' market is another story. There, in the heart of summer, I can get small, crisp okra pods, bright green and unblemished. And by some foresight of nature, they're available at the same time as corn and tomatoes, okra's favorite partners.

Many people have a hard time getting past okra's slippery texture, but aficionados appreciate its clean green-bean taste and the way it thickens tomato sauces. If cooked whole, and not overcooked, the pods have a pleasing crunch and no sliminess whatsoever.

To catch the pods when they are small, okra has to be picked at least every other day, if not daily. "We don't pick on Sunday, and we've always lost some by Monday," says California grower Dru Rivers. At Rivers's Full Belly Farm, the okra goes straight into a cooler and to the farmers' market the following day.

selection: The best okra is small okra, no more than three inches long. The pods should feel tender, yet crisp and snappy, and the stem end should be moist. Avoid pods that feel fibrous or woody. You may also find a beautiful red-podded okra at farmers' markets. Rivers says it can be picked a little bigger than green okra without being woody. Unfortunately, the stunning color changes to green when the okra is cooked.

storage: Okra does not store well. Try to use it within a day or two of buying it, refrigerating it in a paper bag.

onions

California onion grower Wayne Ferrari says he lunches often in summer on salads of sliced red onion, tomato and Armenian cucumber with olive oil and wine vinegar. It's a short-lived pleasure, however. Within a couple of months, these moist new onions develop tough skins and start to sprout.

Most supermarket shoppers are used to storage onions, with their tough, tight outer skins and pungent flavor. But sweet summer onions, yellow or red, are a different experience. They are moist, which is why they don't store well, and although they don't necessarily have more sugar than storage onions, they do have less of the sulfur compounds that make a hot onion hot.

When you shop at the farmers' market in summer, look for these thin-skinned freshly dug onions and take advantage of their brief season. The farmers' market is also a good source for other specialty onions that rarely make it to grocery stores. Watch for cipolline, small squat Italian onions with papery brown skins. Italians like to braise these disklike onions in olive oil with sugar and vinegar. In spring, you may find true spring onions—bulbing onions pulled before the bulb forms. Spring onions look something like leeks but have an even milder taste. Red spring onions are particularly beautiful.

selection: We think of onions as virtually indestructible, but they are perishable—the early, sweet summer onions much more so than the late-summer, sturdy-skinned storage onions. All onions should feel firm and show no sign of mold or sprouting.

storage: Store sweet and storage onions in a cool, dry place with good air circulation. If possible, don't stack them. Store spring onions in a plastic bag in the refrigerator crisper.

peaches

Grower Al Courchesne calls them "sink peaches"—the ones that are so juicy that you have to eat them over the sink. Shoppers who buy fruit from Courchesne's Frog Hollow Farm at Northern California farmers' markets have probably had the sink-peach experience, because Courchesne goes to great trouble to pick his fruit tree-ripe.

The clue to ripeness is the background color, says the grower. It should be golden yellow, with no hint of green. Peaches removed from the tree before they reach that stage—most peaches, in other words—don't have the chance to achieve optimum sugar or texture.

When you grow for farmers' markets and are willing to take extra care in the harvesting and packing, you can grow peaches bred for flavor, not for durability. Over the years, Courchesne has settled on some favorites. Among white peaches, he prefers the Babcock. He calls the crimson red O'Henry "the Cadillac of peaches," but his highest praise goes to the late-season Cal Red, which he lauds for its exquisite flavor. The Mercedes of peaches?

selection: Peaches left on the tree go from greenish yellow, to pale yellow, to full yellow, to golden yellow, with or without a red blush. You want the golden yellow ones. Peaches should be firm but with a little give. Aroma reveals a lot, too. A peach without perfume will almost always lack flavor.

storage: If peaches are firm, leave at room temperature and they will soften over several days. If the fruit is dead-ripe, refrigerate.

plums

Plum grower Gene Etheridge says most shoppers would pass up his best-tasting plum if he weren't right there at the farmers' market urging them to taste it. He's a fan of the Kelsey, "the sweetest plum you can get," insists Etheridge, "but people won't buy them because they're ugly." By sampling and hand-selling, he has introduced countless Southern California shoppers to this prize of a plum.

The same goes for the French Prune plum, a small variety that tastes best when it's wrinkled and prunelike. "People don't realize that looks is not the gauge by which you choose fruit," explains Etheridge. "At the store, you have beautiful-looking fruit; but many times, the box they came in tastes better."

The problem, says the grower, is that many farmers pick their plums hard and under-ripe and let them "self-ripen" in cold storage. But that's a misnomer. Plums don't ripen off the tree. The fruit may get softer, but it won't develop more sugar.

That's why it's a lot more fun to sell at the farmers' market, where people expect tree-ripened fruit. As a general rule, says the grower, the light-skinned varieties are sweeter, but they don't fit people's idea of what a plum should look like. Once they taste them, how-ever, shoppers snap up the supersweet Catalina, the aptly named Elephant Heart (a nearly fist-sized asymetrical plum with blood red flesh), and the sweet, old-fashioned Green Gage.

selection: Whatever the color the plum is meant to be, it should be that color uniformly. A ripe plum has an aroma that makes you want to eat it, says Etheridge, although green-skinned plums tend to have less perfume than dark ones. Plums also should have some "spring"—when you press them gently, they bounce back.

storage: Store ripe plums in the refrigerator. Hard fruit will soften—although not sweeten—on a countertop.

potatoes

It's a pity that many people think the potato world ends with what they find at the super-market. Farmers' market shoppers know better, because in summer they get a glimpse of this vegetable's variety. Some growers plant a dozen different types or more, encouraged by customers' open-mindedness and by the knowledge that potatoes grown for farmers' mar-kets don't have to ship or store well or have uniform appearance.

Northern California grower Wallace Condon, proprietor of Small Potatoes farm, never tires of talking about the potatoes he has grown, the potatoes he is growing and the pota-toes he intends to grow. Not surprisingly, he has clear favorites, many of which you may find at your own farmers' market.

Fingerling potatoes—elongated like fingers and generally thin skinned—are renowned for their firm, waxy texture. Because they hold together when sliced, they make superior potato salad. Among fingerlings, Condon particularly likes Rose Finn Apple, Ruby Crescent and Russian Banana. All three are yellow-fleshed waxy potatoes meant for boiling, steaming or roasting.

Look also for yellow-fleshed potatoes that aren't fingerlings. Yellow Finns not only look as if they've been buttered, they actually taste buttery. Also try Yukon Gold, Bintje or German Butterball. You can bake, steam, fry, saute or boil and mash these potatoes. Their flesh is neither as waxy as the fingerlings nor as fluffy as a russet, but in between.

Another important determinant of eating quality is how long the potato has been in storage. "That's one of the reasons for my success," says Condon. "We dig on Thursday and Friday and sell on Saturday. They're not stored." Potatoes dry out in storage and their fresh-dug flavor evaporates. By shopping at farmers' markets, where you can ask when the potatoes were dug, you have a chance to find out why people make a fuss over "new potatoes."

selection: As a general rule, says Condon, small potatoes tend to have better flavor and texture than large ones. It's not easy to recognize a storage potato, but some signs are dry, chapped or scuffed skin. Avoid potatoes that show signs of sprouting. To get the right variety for your purposes, seek the grower's advice.

storage: Keep potatoes cool, moist and dark, in a paper bag, for example. Don't store them in plastic, and don't refrigerate. Marble-sized potatoes tend to deteriorate quickly. Buy and use within a few days.

summer squashes

The small, firm, fresh-picked zucchini that I can buy direct from growers in summer have none of the bitter taste or watery texture that so often disappoint me in store-bought squashes. The skins are thin, the flesh creamy, the flavor delicate and sweet.

That's because they're fresh, says Doreen Lum, a longtime squash grower in Northern California. Even bigger squashes taste sweet and mild when they're just off the vine. The quality difference is striking, but perhaps not surprising. "A lot of the squashes in supermarkets are a good two weeks old," says Lum.

In addition to the familiar elongated green zucchini, look for golden zucchini, pale green Middle Eastern zucchini, small round French zucchini, and the striped Italian cocozelle. Yellow crookneck squashes need no explaining, but you may be less familiar with the scallop types: pale green pattypan, dark green Scallopini, or golden yellow Sunburst. These beautiful squashes in their vivid colors offer the possibility of some eye-catching combinations with corn and tomatoes.

More and more growers are also bringing squash blossoms to market, sometimes still attached to the baby squash. The flowers are so fragile, says Lum, that her workers pick them at the crack of dawn on market day, harvesting as soon as they can see. These delicate blossoms have a subtle, slightly peppery taste. Stuff them with mozzarella and fry them; or slice, saute in olive oil and toss with pasta and fried zucchini.

selection: The stem end of a squash will tell you how fresh it is. "If you can see a little juice coming out of the stem, it's nice and fresh," says Lum. Avoid limp or excessively scratched squashes. Squash blossoms should be bright, perky and dry.

storage: Keep squashes in a plastic bag in the warmest part of your refrigerator. If you buy baby squashes with blossoms attached, refrigerate them in a plastic bag but leave it open so they get some air. Detached blossoms should be sprinkled with a few drops of water, covered with a damp paper towel and refrigerated.

tomatoes

It is commonplace to complain about supermarket tomatoes and to reminisce, if you're old enough, about the way tomatoes used to be. By now, most shoppers know that supermarkets and their distributors—businesses that depend on moving large volumes—can't give vine-ripened tomatoes the special handling they need. And they recognize that farmers who grow tomatoes for supermarkets must therefore choose varieties that can withstand high-impact shipping. Sadly, flavor and shippability rarely go hand in hand.

But thanks to the proliferation of farmers' markets, consumers have a choice. At markets around the country, growers are showing off stunning tomatoes in a rainbow of colors and a cascade of shapes, sizes and flavors. At many stalls, parents and children stand in line for comparative tastings and sample green-when-ripe Green Zebra tomatoes, tiny Red Currant tomatoes and the prized Amish heirloom tomato called Brandywine.

"It's a wonderful place for consumer education," says Kathleen Barsotti of Capay Fruits & Vegetables, a Northern California tomato grower. Barsotti knows that she can bring unusual tomatoes to the market, and as long as they taste good, people will buy them. Among her favorites are Early Girl and Ace, both red slicing tomatoes; Marvel Stripe, a gold-and-red-striped heirloom tomato; the purple-red Brandywine; the meaty Viva paste tomato; the irresistible Sweet 100 cherry tomato and a new golden orange cherry tomato called Sungold that sells about as fast as farmers can get the baskets on the table.

selection: Ask for a sample if the aroma alone doesn't persuade you of a tomato's flavor. A tomato should smell good and feel firm (not hard), although Barsotti says some heirloom tomatoes get a little soft on top when ripe. The color, whatever it is, should be full and rich. Cosmetic cracking doesn't matter.

storage: Never refrigerate tomatoes unless they are veering toward overripe. (Even then, it would be better just to eat them.) Keep them at room temperature, preferably not in a sunny window where they can get too hot.

summer
RECIPES

blackberry macaroon torte

Among the things my husband brought to our marriage was a copy of *The Cordon Bleu Cook Book* by Dione Lucas, copyright 1947. He claims to have made several dishes from it in his bachelor days, but the only one he ever made for me is the layered summer fruit torte—Lucas called it a *vacherin*—on which this recipe is based. The crisp layers are baked nut meringues in thin rounds; the soft layers are whipped cream and ripe fruit—blackberries, in this case, but you could also use strawberries, peaches or nectarines.

WHITES OF 3 LARGE EGGS

½ CUP SUGAR

6 TABLESPOONS FINELY GROUND TOASTED ALMONDS (SEE NOTE)

2 TABLESPOONS UNSALTED BUTTER, MELTED AND COOLED

3 TABLESPOONS SIFTED UNBLEACHED ALL-PURPOSE FLOUR

1 POUND BLACKBERRIES

3 TABLESPOONS VANILLA SUGAR (SEE NOTE)

3 TABLESPOONS BRANDY

1 CUP HEAVY CREAM

SERVES 4

NOTES: To toast almonds, preheat oven to 350 degrees F. Toast ½ cup whole unblanched almonds on a baking sheet until lightly colored inside. (Break one open to check.) Cool, then grind fine—but not to a paste—in a small food processor or nut grinder. You will have a little more than 6 tablespoons. To make vanilla sugar, put a whole vanilla bean in a closed canister of sugar and shake canister occasionally to redistribute the bean. Within a week, the sugar will be infused with vanilla flavor. You can keep adding sugar to replace the sugar you use until the bean starts to lose its pungency.

Line 2 heavy baking sheets with parchment paper. Using an overturned plate or a cardboard template, trace 3 rounds (2 on one sheet, 1 on the other) each about 7½ inches in diameter. Position 2 racks in the center of the oven. Preheat oven to 350 degrees F.

Beat egg whites to firm but not stiff peaks. Add sugar gradually, whisking constantly to make a soft meringue. Whisk until mixture no longer tastes grainy. Carefully fold in nuts, then butter, then flour. Divide mixture evenly among the 3 rounds, spreading each to an even thickness. Bake until lightly and evenly browned, about 30 minutes, switching position of trays halfway through. Carefully transfer the parchment sheets to a rack to cool. When cool, peel off parchment.

In a bowl, combine blackberries, 2 tablespoons vanilla sugar and 1 tablespoon brandy. Toss well and let berries stand 15 minutes.

In another bowl, whisk cream to soft peaks. Add remaining tablespoon vanilla sugar and 2 tablespoons brandy and whisk briefly just to blend.

To assemble the torte: Put 1 macaroon layer on a cake plate or stand. Top with one-third of the whipped cream, spreading it evenly. Set aside several berries to garnish the top, then put half of the remaining berries on the cream-covered macaroon, spreading them evenly. Top with another macaroon, pressing on it gently to make it level. Spread the surface (not the sides) with half of the remaining whipped cream and top with all but the reserved berries, again spreading evenly. Top with remaining macaroon and whipped cream. Garnish with reserved berries.

You can serve it immediately but I like to let it stand about 30 minutes to soften the macaroons slightly. Refrigerate if weather is warm or if you are letting it stand longer than 30 minutes. Depending on how juicy the berries are, the torte can stand for an hour or two. To serve, slice into wedges with a sharp knife.

cucumber, arugula and red onion salad with goat cheese toasts

The skinny, dark green Japanese cucumbers are so crisp and sweet that they don't need salting to rid them of bitter juices. For an easy first course, cut the cucumbers in chunks and serve them with tomato wedges, black olives, feta cheese, olive oil and coarse salt.

The following recipe is almost equally simple and refreshing. Just be sure not to salt the cucumbers until you are ready to serve them or the salt will wilt them and thin out your dressing. For the toasts, choose a fresh goat cheese with no rind.

1 BAGUETTE

1 TABLESPOON PLUS 1 TEASPOON EXTRA VIRGIN OLIVE OIL

3 OUNCES FRESH GOAT CHEESE, IN ONE PIECE

FOR THE SALAD:

¾ POUND JAPANESE CUCUMBERS, PEELED IF DESIRED, AND VERY THINLY SLICED

½ RED ONION, VERY THINLY SLICED

1 CLOVE GARLIC, MINCED

1 TABLESPOON WALNUT OIL

1 TABLESPOON EXTRA VIRGIN OLIVE OIL

2½ TO 3 TEASPOONS WHITE WINE VINEGAR

SALT AND FRESHLY GROUND BLACK PEPPER

¼ POUND YOUNG ARUGULA

18 NIÇOISE OLIVES

SERVES 6

Preheat oven to 425 degrees F. Cut the baguette on a severe diagonal into 6 thin slices about 7 to 8 inches long and about ¼ inch thick. Save leftover baguette for another use. Using 1 tablespoon olive oil, brush both sides of the baguette slices. Arrange on a baking sheet and bake until golden, about 15 minutes. Remove from oven and set aside. Reduce oven heat to 375 degrees F.

Put goat cheese in a small baking dish and top with remaining teaspoon olive oil. Bake until it is quite warm and soft to the touch, 6 to 8 minutes.

While cheese bakes, make the salad: In a large bowl, combine cucumbers, onion, garlic, walnut oil, olive oil and 2½ teaspoons

(CONTINUED)

vinegar. Season to taste with salt and pepper and toss well. Add arugula and toss again gently. Taste and adjust seasoning, adding another ½ teaspoon vinegar if needed.

Arrange salad on a serving platter. Scatter olives over the top and around the edge. Spread warm cheese on toasts, then place toasts around salad or pass separately.

roasted corn soup

When you have temporarily had your fill of corn on the cob from the farmers' market, turn a few of those succulent ears into corn soup. My recipe is adapted from one given to me by Mary Evely, the chef at Simi Winery in Healdsburg, California. Roasting the ears first contributes a subtle nuttiness, so the soup isn't tiresomely sweet. Mary also uses a little potato and cornmeal to give the soup body. The finished puree is a rich sunflower color. You could drizzle the surface with basil oil or crème fraîche, but it is also lovely and pure just as it is.

6 EARS CORN, PREFERABLY NOT SUPERSWEET VARIETIES, WITH HUSKS INTACT

3 LARGE CLOVES GARLIC, UNPEELED

2 CUPS HOMEMADE OR CANNED LOW-SODIUM CHICKEN BROTH

1 BAKING POTATO (ABOUT ½ POUND), PEELED, IN 6 PIECES

1 TABLESPOON CORNMEAL

½ CUP HEAVY CREAM

SALT AND FRESHLY GROUND BLACK PEPPER

PINCH SUGAR, OPTIONAL

MAKES ABOUT 7½ CUPS, TO SERVE 6

Preheat oven to 450 degrees F. Put unhusked corn and unpeeled garlic on a baking sheet and roast until corn is fragrant and husks are lightly browned, about 25 minutes. Let cool, then remove husks and silks. Cut kernels away from cobs. Cut 4 cobs in half crosswise with a heavy knife or cleaver. Discard remaining 2 cobs. Peel the garlic. Set corn kernels and garlic cloves aside.

In a saucepan, combine broth, potato, the halved corn cobs and 3 cups water. Cover partially, bring to a simmer over moderate heat and adjust heat to maintain a simmer. Cook until potato pieces are tender, about 20 minutes. Discard corn cobs.

In a food processor, combine corn kernels, garlic cloves, potatoes (lift them out of the broth with a slotted spoon) and cornmeal. Puree, adding potato broth gradually through the feed tube. Transfer soup to a sieve set over a bowl and press mixture through sieve with a rubber spatula, leaving corn skins behind.

Transfer soup to a clean saucepan. Stir in cream and reheat. Season to taste with salt, pepper and a pinch of sugar, if desired.

pasta with eggplant, tomato, olives and capers

There's no end to the pasta sauces built on eggplant and tomato, vegetables nature brings together at the farmers' market. Unfortunately, frying the eggplant in a lot of oil is often step number one. I particularly like the following alternative, which uses roasted eggplant. The cooked and chopped eggplant is simmered with tomato sauce until the two blend well, then enlivened with olives and capers. A short pasta shape with curves or grooves—such as gemelli or fusilli —will hold the sauce nicely; if you can't find either, use penne or mezzi rigatoni. The sauce can be made a day ahead. Note that it requires a food mill.

1 POUND ITALIAN OR JAPANESE EGGPLANTS
¼ CUP EXTRA VIRGIN OLIVE OIL
½ LARGE ONION, MINCED
1 CARROT, DICED
1 CELERY RIB, DICED
PINCH HOT RED PEPPER FLAKES
4 CLOVES GARLIC, MINCED
1 TABLESPOON CHOPPED ITALIAN PARSLEY
1½ POUNDS PLUM TOMATOES, DICED
SALT
PINCH SUGAR, OPTIONAL
1 DOZEN FRESH BASIL LEAVES
1 TABLESPOON CAPERS
¼ CUP COARSELY CHOPPED IMPORTED BLACK OLIVES SUCH AS NIÇOISE OR GAETA
1½ POUNDS DRIED GEMELLI, FUSILLI OR PENNE
FRESHLY GRATED PECORINO ROMANO CHEESE

SERVES 6 TO 8

Preheat oven to 425 degrees F. Prick eggplants in several places with a sharp knife, then arrange on a heavy baking sheet. Bake until completely soft, about 50 minutes. When cool, cut in half lengthwise. Scrape out the flesh and discard the skins. Chop the flesh very fine.

Heat olive oil in a 12-inch skillet over moderate heat. Add onion, carrot and celery and saute until very soft, about 15 minutes. Add hot-pepper flakes, garlic and parsley and saute 1 minute to release garlic fragrance. Add tomatoes and salt to taste and cook, stirring often, until tomatoes collapse and form a thick and tasty sauce, about 20 minutes. Add water as needed to keep sauce from becoming too thick. Taste and add sugar if tomatoes seem a little tart.

Pass tomato sauce through a food mill and return to skillet. Stir in eggplant and basil. Simmer, stirring often, until flavors are well blended and sauce is tasty, about 5 minutes, adding water as needed to keep sauce from drying out. Stir in capers and olives. Keep warm over low heat.

Bring a large pot of salted water to a boil over high heat. Add pasta and cook until al dente. Drain, reserving about 1 cup of the cooking water. Return pasta to pot and add the sauce. Toss well, adding a little of the reserved water if needed to thin the sauce. Transfer to warm plates. Top each with a little cheese, passing additional cheese at the table.

pasta shop's roasted eggplant salad

On the cusp of summer and fall, the farmers' market offers three vegetables dear to Mediterranean cooks: tomatoes, eggplants and sweet peppers. From Moroccan eggplant salad with tomato and peppers to Lebanese *alib batinjan*, a stew of the three vegetables with mint, the combinations know no end. Here's a California contribution to the repertoire, a popular salad from the Pasta Shop in Oakland, California. I think it is best when it has rested for a few hours, allowing the flavors to blend. Make it in the morning for an afternoon picnic, or in mid-afternoon for a dinner with grilled chicken or lamb.

1½ POUNDS JAPANESE OR ITALIAN EGGPLANTS

6 TABLESPOONS PLUS 2 TEASPOONS EXTRA VIRGIN OLIVE OIL

SALT AND FRESHLY GROUND BLACK PEPPER

1 HEAD GARLIC

1 RED BELL PEPPER

1 GOLDEN BELL PEPPER

½ GREEN BELL PEPPER

1 LARGE RED ONION

½ POUND CHERRY TOMATOES, HALVED

¼ CUP COARSELY CHOPPED ITALIAN PARSLEY

2 TABLESPOONS RED WINE VINEGAR

2 TABLESPOONS BALSAMIC VINEGAR

SERVES 6

Preheat oven to 425 degrees F. Cut eggplants in half lengthwise, then in ¾-inch chunks. Place in a bowl and toss with 4 tablespoons oil and salt and pepper to taste; transfer to a heavy baking sheet. Roast until just tender and lightly browned, about 30 minutes, stirring once or twice with a spatula to make sure eggplant chunks aren't sticking to the baking sheet. Transfer to a large, shallow serving bowl.

Meanwhile, with a small knife, cut all around the head of garlic at the "equator," penetrating the paper skin but not the cloves.

Remove the papery outer layers from the top half of the head (opposite the roots), exposing the cloves. Place garlic on a large square of aluminum foil and drizzle with 2 teaspoons olive oil. Loosely wrap the foil around it, sealing edges tightly. Slip garlic into oven alongside eggplants and bake until cloves are soft, about 45 minutes.

Remove seeds and ribs from bell peppers. Cut peppers and onion in 1-inch pieces. In a large skillet, heat remaining 2 tablespoons olive oil over high heat. Add bell peppers and onions, season with salt and pepper and saute until tender but not mushy, 8 to 10 minutes. Transfer to bowl with eggplant. Add cherry tomatoes to skillet, season with salt and pepper and saute just to heat them through, about 1 minute; do not let them lose their shape. Transfer to bowl with eggplant and add parsley.

Squeeze the softened garlic out of the skins into a small bowl and mash to a puree. Whisk in vinegars. Pour about three-fourths of the mixture over the vegetables and toss gently, taking care not to break up the eggplant. Taste and add more of the vinegar mixture, salt or pepper if necessary. Serve at room temperature.

fresh fig galettes

If I lived closer to Healdsburg, California, I would start every summer Saturday the same way: with a visit to the charming farmers' market, followed by a stop at the Downtown Bakery on the town's main square for a warm fruit galette and a cup of coffee. I'd like to think my attempt at re-creating the bakery's extraordinary galettes is not too far off the mark.

These are individual rustic tarts that shouldn't look too polished or fancy—perfect for amateur bakers, like myself, who have never mastered the art of the elegantly crimped pie shell. They may be humble, but they are beautiful, with the dark purple skin of the figs outlining the rosy red flesh, and with sugar glistening on the rims. In season, use the same recipe to make galettes of peaches, apricots, plums or mixed fruits.

FOR THE DOUGH:

2 CUPS UNBLEACHED ALL-PURPOSE FLOUR

¾ TEASPOON SALT

½ CUP UNSALTED BUTTER, CHILLED, IN SMALL PIECES

7 TABLESPOONS SOLID VEGETABLE SHORTENING, CHILLED, IN SMALL PIECES

APPROXIMATELY ¼ CUP ICE WATER

FOR THE FILLING:

1½ POUNDS FRESH FIGS

6 TABLESPOONS SUGAR (OR LESS IF FRUIT IS QUITE RIPE)

EGG WASH: 1 EGG YOLK WHISKED WITH 2 TEASPOONS HEAVY CREAM

SUGAR, FOR GALETTE RIMS

MAKES 6 GALETTES, TO SERVE 6

90

To make the dough: In a food processor, combine flour and salt. Pulse three or four times to blend. Add butter pieces and pulse a few times, just until fat is evenly distributed and coated with flour. Add shortening pieces and pulse a few times, just until fat is coated with flour. There should still be pieces of flour-coated fat about the size of large peas. Transfer the mixture to a large bowl. Drizzle with ice water while tossing with a fork just until it begins to come together into clumps, then gather the dough together with your hands. You may have to knead it slightly to get it to hold together, but that's better than adding more water. Handle dough as little as possible, then wrap it in plastic wrap and refrigerate until chilled, at least 2 hours.

Preheat oven to 425 degrees F.

To make the filling: Quarter figs through the stem end or, if large, cut them in sixths. Set aside in a bowl. Just before you are ready to assemble the galettes, sprinkle the figs with 6 tablespoons sugar and toss gently to distribute.

Divide dough in 6 equal pieces. Working with 1 piece at a time, roll dough out on a lightly floured board into a circle about ⅛-inch thick. Use an upturned plate or a cardboard template to trace a neat 7-inch circle. Transfer circle to a heavy baking sheet. Arrange one-sixth of the figs attractively in the center, leaving a 1½-inch edge all the way around. Fold the edge over to create a border, making sure there are no cracks in the dough or the

(CONTINUED)

fruit juices will seep out during baking. Patch, if necessary, with bits of trimmed dough lightly moistened with cold water.

Brush the border with a little egg wash, then sprinkle the border generously with sugar. Repeat with remaining dough to make 6 galettes. You will probably be able to fit only half of them on the baking sheet at a time. If you have only 1 oven, assemble and bake 3 galettes at a time rather than bake 2 sheets at once. Bake until crust is golden and fruit is bubbly, 22 to 25 minutes. Transfer to a rack and cool slightly before serving.

yard-long beans with tomato, ginger and chile

A farmers' market is a great place to buy unfamiliar vegetables because you can usually get some cooking advice with your purchase. Any long-bean grower will tell you, for example, that these beans should be braised, not boiled. They may look delicate, because they are slender, but their flavor really develops when they are cooked at length. (Chinese cooks also deep-fry them first, then braise them briefly.) The following preparation is absolutely better made a day ahead and left to absorb the seasonings. The beans could be a side dish for chicken, duck or pork, but I typically eat them on their own, as a simple dinner with steamed basmati rice.

2 TABLESPOONS VEGETABLE OIL
SCANT ½ TEASPOON CUMIN SEEDS
2 LARGE CLOVES GARLIC, MINCED
1 TABLESPOON FINELY MINCED
FRESH GINGER
1 JALAPEÑO CHILE, HALVED
¾ POUND FRESH PLUM TOMATOES,
FINELY CHOPPED
1 POUND YARD-LONG BEANS, ENDS
TRIMMED, IN 4-INCH LENGTHS
½ CUP CHOPPED CILANTRO
SALT

SERVES 4

Heat a large skillet or wok over high heat. When hot, add oil. When oil is hot, add cumin seeds. Stand back, as they may sputter and pop. When they begin to release their fragrance, add the garlic, ginger and chile. Stir-fry until seasonings begin to color, about 1 minute, then add tomatoes. Cook over high heat, stirring often, until tomatoes collapse and begin to form a thick sauce, about 5 minutes. Add a little water as needed to keep tomatoes from sticking. Add beans, cilantro and ¼ cup water. Season well with salt.

Cover, reduce heat to maintain a simmer and cook until beans are tender, about 1 hour, adding more water as needed to keep beans from sticking. Remove chile before serving.

green bean salad with cherry tomatoes and ricotta salata

Tender, sweet and delicate, the elegant green filet beans (also known as *haricots verts*) deserve to be a centerpiece of summer meals. They are never inexpensive, but when you find them at the farmers' market with sweet summer red onions and great cherry tomatoes, you have the makings of a salad that will repay your investment. If you can't find ricotta salata, a sliceable Italian sheep's milk cheese, use Greek manouri or any young sheep's milk cheese firm enough to shave into pale flakes with a cheese plane.

FOR THE DRESSING:

¼ CUP EXTRA VIRGIN OLIVE OIL

1 TABLESPOON PLUS 2 TEASPOONS WHITE WINE VINEGAR

SALT AND FRESHLY GROUND BLACK PEPPER

½ RED ONION, MINCED

ICE WATER

1 POUND GREEN FILET BEANS (*HARICOTS VERTS*), ENDS TRIMMED

½ POUND SMALL CHERRY TOMATOES, PREFERABLY MIXED RED AND GOLD VARIETIES, HALVED

2 OUNCES RICOTTA SALATA CHEESE

SERVES 6

To make the dressing: In a large bowl, whisk together olive oil, wine vinegar and salt and pepper to taste. (Beans need a lot of salt.) Whisk in onion, then set dressing aside.

Have ready a bowl of ice water. Bring a large pot of salted water to a boil over high heat. Add beans and cook until crisp-tender, about 5 minutes. Drain in a sieve or colander, then transfer to the ice water to stop the cooking. When beans are cool, drain again and pat thoroughly dry with a clean dish towel.

Add beans to bowl with dressing and toss to coat. Add tomatoes and toss again. With a cheese plane, shave the cheese directly into the bowl in paper-thin slices. Toss again gently to keep the flakes in large pieces, then transfer salad to a shallow serving platter.

green beans with turnips

The skinny French beans called *haricots verts* (or, sometimes, filet beans) are unmatched for flavor and tenderness—but only when slender. If they are even as big around as a pencil, they will be tough. Because they grow quickly, growers have to harvest daily to get them at just the right moment. Blanched briefly, then tossed with young braised turnips and butter, they are a true delicacy. Serve as a first course or an accompaniment to pork or lamb.

1½ TABLESPOONS UNSALTED BUTTER

¾ POUND BABY TURNIPS, THICKLY PEELED AND CUT IN HALVES, QUARTERS OR SIXTHS, DEPENDING ON SIZE

SALT AND FRESHLY GROUND BLACK PEPPER

2 SHALLOTS, MINCED

¾ POUND GREEN FILET BEANS (HARICOTS VERTS), ENDS TRIMMED

1 TABLESPOON MINCED ITALIAN PARSLEY

SERVES 4

Melt butter in a large skillet over moderately low heat. Add turnips, season with salt and pepper and toss to coat with butter. Cover and cook, shaking skillet occasionally, until turnips are just tender and lightly browned in spots, 10 to 15 minutes. Uncover, add shallots and saute 2 minutes to soften the shallots.

While turnips are cooking, bring a large pot of salted water to a boil over high heat. Add beans and cook until crisp-tender, about 5 minutes. Drain well, pat dry, then transfer to skillet with turnips and toss to coat with seasonings. Taste and add more salt and pepper if necessary. (Green beans need a lot of salt.) Add parsley, toss again and serve.

just-like-pauline's pesto pizza

If you call Pauline's Pizza Pie in San Francisco when the restaurant is closed, you get an answering machine with an attitude. You've reached Pauline's, the recording says, home of the best pizza you ever ate. It's the best pesto pizza, in any case. I crave it regularly, although I believe my own recipe is a good imitation. Pauline's secret is to brush the pesto on at the end, after the pizza comes out of the oven. Other key points for home bakers include giving the dough a long, slow rise and using a baking stone or baking tiles for a crisp crust.

Purists say that proper pesto can only be made with the small-leaved, delicately perfumed basil grown around Genoa. Fortunately for purists, American seed companies now offer a Genovese basil and some growers are bringing it to the farmers' market. But I think you will enjoy this pesto made with whatever fresh basil you find, as long as the leaves are in good condition and the plant is not flowering, which tends to make the leaves stronger tasting.

This recipe makes enough pesto for two pizzas. You can double the dough, or you can cover half the pesto with a film of olive oil, refrigerate it and use it on pasta the next day

FOR THE PIZZA DOUGH:

1 ½ TEASPOONS ACTIVE DRY YEAST
¾ CUP WARM WATER
1 TABLESPOON OLIVE OIL
1 TEASPOON SALT
APPROXIMATELY 1¾ CUPS UNBLEACHED ALL-PURPOSE FLOUR

FOR THE PESTO:

3 TABLESPOONS PINE NUTS
1 CUP LIGHTLY PACKED BASIL LEAVES
1 LARGE CLOVE GARLIC, THINLY SLICED
⅓ CUP EXTRA VIRGIN OLIVE OIL
2 TABLESPOONS FRESHLY GRATED PARMESAN CHEESE
SALT

CORNMEAL, FOR DUSTING

⅓ POUND LOW-MOISTURE WHOLE-MILK MOZZARELLA CHEESE, COARSELY GRATED
OLIVE OIL, FOR BRUSHING THE RIM

MAKES ONE 13- TO 14-INCH PIZZA, TO SERVE 2

To make the dough: Sprinkle yeast over warm water in a large bowl and let stand 2 minutes. Stir with a fork to blend. Let stand until bubbly, about 10 minutes. Whisk in olive oil and salt. Add 1 ½ cups flour, stirring with a wooden spoon. Turn dough out onto a lightly floured board and knead until smooth and elastic, 6 to 8 minutes, using as much of the remaining ¼ cup flour as needed to keep dough from sticking to the board or your hands. Shape into a ball, transfer to an oiled bowl, turn dough to coat with oil, then cover tightly with plastic wrap and let rise at room temperature for 2 hours.

(CONTINUED)

96

Punch dough down, reshape into a ball, re-cover the bowl and let dough rise again for 4 hours.

Position a rack in the middle of the oven and line with baking tiles or a baking stone. Preheat to 550 degrees F or highest setting for at least 45 minutes. Punch dough down and turn it out onto a work surface. Shape into a ball. Cover with a clean dish towel and let rest 30 minutes.

To make the pesto: Toast pine nuts on a baking sheet in a 325 degree F oven until they are golden brown, 12 to 15 minutes. Let cool. In a food processor, combine pine nuts, basil and garlic. Pulse, scraping down sides occasionally, until well chopped. With motor running, add oil through feed tube. Transfer mixture to a bowl and stir in cheese and salt to taste. Cover with plastic wrap, pressing directly onto surface to prevent discoloring.

To assemble the pizza: On a lightly floured surface, roll out dough into a 13- to 14-inch round. Transfer to a pizza peel or rimless baking sheet well dusted with cornmeal. Working quickly, spread cheese evenly over dough round, leaving a ¾-inch rim. (If you don't work quickly, the dough may stick to the peel or sheet.) Brush the rim with olive oil.

Immediately slide pizza from peel onto oven tiles or stone and bake until crust is crisp and browned, about 8 minutes. Remove from oven. Immediately brush surface of pizza with pesto, using about half the mixture (see recipe introduction). Brush the rim with olive oil. Serve immediately.

crostini with braised onions and pancetta

It's a shame most cooks think of onions only as a background ingredient, valued for the sweetness they contribute to stews or the crunch they lend to a burger but not worth much attention themselves. Slow-cooked onions become soft, sweet and creamy—a perfect topping for crisp toasts. Serve these warm crostini before dinner with a glass of white wine; a Gewürztraminer would be perfection. You can use yellow or red onions in the recipe; although the red onions lose their bright color and turn slightly gray when cooked, their flavor is superb.

¼ CUP EXTRA VIRGIN OLIVE OIL

2 OUNCES PANCETTA, MINCED

1 POUND YELLOW OR RED ONIONS, HALVED AND THINLY SLICED

3 CLOVES GARLIC, MINCED

1 TEASPOON MINCED FRESH THYME

SALT AND FRESHLY GROUND BLACK PEPPER

8 SLICES COUNTRY-STYLE BREAD, EACH ABOUT ½ INCH THICK AND 4 INCHES LONG

BALSAMIC VINEGAR

1 TABLESPOON MINCED ITALIAN PARSLEY

MAKES 8 TOASTS, TO SERVE 4

Heat 2 tablespoons olive oil and the pancetta in a 10-inch skillet over moderate heat until pancetta just begins to crisp, about 3 minutes. Add onions, garlic, thyme and salt and pepper to taste. Stir well, then cover and cook until onions are soft and sweet, about 15 minutes. Uncover occasionally to make sure onions are not burning, although it adds a pleasing taste if they caramelize slightly.

Preheat broiler or toaster. Toast bread on both sides until lightly colored. Drizzle toasts on one side with remaining 2 tablespoons oil. Top with onions and drizzle lightly with balsamic vinegar. Garnish each toast with some of the minced parsley. Let cool 5 minutes before serving.

chunky peach preserves

Spread on hot biscuits and whole-grain toast, or stir a spoonful into plain yogurt for breakfast. Be sure to sample the peaches at the farmers' market before you commit to three pounds; great jam starts with great fruit.

3 POUNDS FREESTONE PEACHES
SUCH AS ELBERTA
ICE WATER
4½ CUPS SUGAR
⅔ CUP STRAINED FRESH LEMON
JUICE, PLUS MORE TO TASTE

MAKES 3 PINTS

Cut an X in the rounded end of each peach. Bring a saucepan full of water to a boil over high heat. Have ready a bowl of ice water. Add peaches a few at a time to the boiling water and blanch 30 seconds, then transfer to the ice water to stop the cooking. When cool, lift out and peel. The skin should peel back easily from the X.

Cut peaches into wedges about ½ inch thick, then cut each wedge in half crosswise. Transfer to a large bowl, add sugar and lemon juice and stir well. Let stand several hours or overnight, stirring two or three times, until sugar dissolves and mixture no longer tastes grainy.

Transfer to a large pot, bring to a simmer over moderately high heat and simmer, skimming any white foam that collects on the surface, until peaches are tender and syrup thickens slightly, 25 to 30 minutes. Transfer to a large bowl, cover and let rest overnight to "plump" the fruit again.

Drain the fruit in a sieve set over a bowl. Taste the syrup and add more lemon juice if it seems too sweet. Return the syrup to a pot and cook over moderately high heat until it reaches 220 degrees F. Or test for jam-like consistency by spooning a little onto a chilled saucer, then returning the saucer to the freezer for a couple of minutes to cool the syrup quickly. It should firm to a soft jelly consistency.

Return the peaches and any collected juices to the pot and cook a couple of minutes more, until mixture returns to 220 degrees F. It will seem thin. Remove from heat and let stand 5 minutes, then spoon into clean, hot jars to within ½ inch from the top. Wipe rim clean with a towel dipped in hot water. Place lids and rings on jars and seal tightly. Cool and refrigerate for up to 3 months. Or, for longer storage, place just-filled jars in boiling water to cover by 1 inch and boil 15 minutes for half-pint jars, 20 minutes for pint jars. Transfer with tongs to a rack to cool; lids should form a seal. Sealed jars may be stored in a pantry for up to a year.

white peaches in raspberry wine sauce

Thumbing through *The Natural Cuisine of Georges Blanc*, the work of the renowned French chef, I was smitten by a picture of white peaches in raspberry sauce served in a wineglass. The reflection of a magnificent chateau shimmers in the glass, and you want to reach out and pull the dessert off the page. Fortunately, American farmers' markets offer sumptuous white peaches and fragrant raspberries in summer, so you can make a similar creation yourself. My recipe is a simplification and adaptation of chef Blanc's original, which exploits the harmony between the two summer fruits.

1 CUP WATER
1 CUP DRY WHITE WINE
⅓ CUP SUGAR
1 BOX (1 CUP) RASPBERRIES
1 TABLESPOON COINTREAU, GRAPPA OR MARC
4 WHITE PEACHES SUCH AS BABCOCK

SERVES 8

Combine water, wine and sugar in a saucepan. Bring to a simmer over moderately high heat, stirring to dissolve sugar. Simmer until reduced to ½ cup, 10 to 12 minutes. Refrigerate until cold.

Puree raspberries in a food processor. Then, using a rubber spatula, press puree through a sieve into a bowl. Stir in cold wine syrup and Cointreau or other liqueur and chill.

To serve, put 2 tablespoons raspberry syrup in each of 8 balloon wineglasses. Peel the peaches. (If they are ripe, the skin should peel back easily with a paring knife.) Slice and divide among the wineglasses. Serve immediately.

fingerling potato salad with fennel

You need a waxy potato for potato salad, and my favorite are fingerlings—so called because they are long and slender, like fingers. They have a waxy texture when cooked, so the potatoes don't crumble when cut. If you can't find them, ask your grower about his or her best potatoes for salad. For a picnic, a sandwich lunch or an accompaniment to grilled salmon, toss the boiled potatoes with sliced fennel, chervil and a shallot vinaigrette.

FOR THE VINAIGRETTE:

2 SHALLOTS, MINCED

1 TABLESPOON CHAMPAGNE OR WHITE WINE VINEGAR, OR MORE TO TASTE

3 TABLESPOONS EXTRA VIRGIN OLIVE OIL

SALT AND FRESHLY GROUND BLACK PEPPER

1 POUND FINGERLING POTATOES OR OTHER WAXY NEW POTATOES

2 TABLESPOONS CHOPPED FRESH CHERVIL OR PARSLEY

½ SMALL FENNEL BULB, STALKS REMOVED

SERVES 4

To make the vinaigrette: In a small bowl, whisk together shallots, 1 tablespoon vinegar and olive oil. Season to taste with salt and pepper. Set aside for 20 minutes to marry flavors.

Put potatoes in a large saucepan with salted water to cover. Bring to a boil over high heat, then adjust heat to maintain a simmer. Cover partially and cook until a knife pierces the potatoes easily, 12 to 15 minutes. Drain and peel while hot. Slice potatoes about ¼ inch thick. Transfer to a large bowl, add half the vinaigrette (about 2 tablespoons) and 1 tablespoon chervil and toss gently to coat. Taste and adjust seasoning.

Cut fennel bulb in half to make 2 wedges. Cut away the core. Slice wedges crosswise as thinly as possible. (A mandoline or other manual vegetable slicer is helpful.) In a bowl, combine fennel with remaining vinaigrette and remaining tablespoon chervil. Toss gently, then taste and adjust seasoning.

One hour before serving, combine potatoes and fennel and toss gently. Taste and adjust seasoning. It may need more salt.

grilled zucchini with tomato and olive salad

Sliced lengthwise and charcoal grilled with olive oil and thyme, zucchini are so appetizing that I want to eat them right off the grill. Arranged on a platter and topped with a mixture of diced tomato, black olives, capers and hand-torn basil, they make an enticing first course. Or, serve with grilled lamb, tuna or swordfish.

1 POUND ZUCCHINI

2 TABLESPOONS EXTRA VIRGIN OLIVE OIL

1½ TEASPOONS MINCED FRESH THYME

⅓ POUND TOMATOES, IN NEAT, SMALL DICE

1 LARGE CLOVE GARLIC, MINCED

2 DOZEN NIÇOISE OLIVES, PITTED

1 TABLESPOON COARSELY CHOPPED CAPERS

1½ TEASPOONS RED WINE VINEGAR

SALT AND FRESHLY GROUND BLACK PEPPER

8 TO 10 FRESH BASIL LEAVES

Prepare a hot charcoal fire. Cut zucchini lengthwise into slices about ¼ inch thick. Put them on a large platter or baking sheet, drizzle with 1 tablespoon olive oil and sprinkle with thyme. Toss with your hands to coat them evenly with oil and herbs.

In a small bowl, combine tomatoes, garlic, olives, capers, wine vinegar and remaining tablespoon olive oil. Set aside.

Just before coals are ready, season zucchini with salt and pepper. Grill on both sides until browned, about 3 minutes per side. Transfer to a large serving platter, arranging them in a single layer. Season tomato mixture with salt and pepper, then spoon it on top, spreading it evenly over the zucchini. Tear the basil leaves and scatter over the surface. Serve immediately.

103

SERVES 4

farmers' market greek salad

Imagine how stunning a Greek salad would be if it were made with just-picked, flavor-packed ingredients from a farmers' market: sugar-sweet cherry tomatoes and slicing tomatoes in red, yellow and green; small, crisp cucumbers that don't even need peeling; new-crop red onions and vibrant green or purple basil. Layered with shiny black olives and crumbled feta cheese, these raw ingredients make one of the world's most inviting salads.

1 POUND MIXED TOMATOES, IN DIF-
FERENT COLORS AND SIZES,
INCLUDING SOME CHERRY TOMA-
TOES, BOTH RED AND GOLD

¼ RED ONION, SLICED PAPER-THIN

1 SMALL JAPANESE OR 2 MEDITER-
RANEAN CUCUMBERS, ABOUT ⅓
POUND TOTAL WEIGHT, THINLY
SLICED

2 OUNCES FETA CHEESE, PREFER-
ABLY GREEK OR BULGARIAN

10 TO 12 FRESH BASIL LEAVES

SALT AND FRESHLY GROUND
BLACK PEPPER

16 KALAMATA OLIVES

2 TABLESPOONS EXTRA VIRGIN
OLIVE OIL

1 TABLESPOON WHITE WINE VIN-
EGAR

1 LARGE CLOVE GARLIC, MINCED TO
A PASTE WITH SALT

Core and halve the large tomatoes through the stem, then lay cut side down and slice into half-rounds. Halve the cherry tomatoes. Arrange the large tomatoes on a platter, alternating the colors attractively. Top with onion, then with cucumber rounds. Sprinkle the halved cherry tomatoes on top of the cucumbers. Dot the surface with small clumps of cheese. Tear basil leaves into small pieces and scatter over all. Season with salt and pepper. Arrange the olives around the edge of the platter.

In a small bowl, whisk together olive oil, wine vinegar and garlic. Season with salt and pepper. Pour over salad just before serving.

**SERVES 4 AS A FIRST COURSE, 2 AS
A LUNCH MAIN COURSE**

quesadillas with squash blossoms and corn

More frequently now, farmers are bringing baby zucchini to market with their blossoms still attached. The beautiful green-and-gold flowers can be stuffed with cheese, then battered and fried; or, as here, they can be shredded and added to a quesadilla filling. Like the edible flowers tossed into salads, they are more an amusement than an identifiable flavor, although they do have a subtle peppery taste. If I find the flowers with the vegetable attached, I like to steam the zucchini separately and serve them whole, dressed with extra virgin olive oil and coarse salt.

If possible, use two skillets to make two quesadillas at a time. They should be served and eaten immediately. The salsa ingredients can be chopped ahead of time, but combine them at the last minute so the mixture doesn't get watery.

¼ POUND SQUASH BLOSSOMS

2 TABLESPOONS VEGETABLE OIL, PLUS MORE FOR FRYING QUESADIL-LAS

1 SMALL ONION, MINCED

1 CLOVE GARLIC, MINCED

SALT AND FRESHLY GROUND BLACK PEPPER

½ CUP CORN KERNELS

4 FLOUR TORTILLAS, EACH 10 INCHES IN DIAMETER

¾ POUND LOW-MOISTURE WHOLE-MILK MOZZARELLA OR MONTEREY JACK, GRATED

FOR THE SALSA CRUDA:

1 LARGE TOMATO, FINELY DICED

½ MEDIUM ONION, FINELY DICED

½ TO 1 JALAPEÑO CHILE, FINELY DICED

1 TABLESPOON MINCED CILANTRO

SALT

MAKES 4 QUESADILLAS, TO SERVE 4

Halve the squash blossoms lengthwise and remove the pistils. If the blossoms are large (more than about 2 inches long and 1 inch wide), cut them in half again. Heat 2 tablespoons vegetable oil in a large skillet over moderate heat. Add onion and garlic and saute until onion is soft, about 10 minutes. Add squash blossoms, season with salt and pepper and saute, stirring gently, until they begin to soften, about 3 minutes. Do not let them wilt. Add the corn, stir gently to blend, then remove from heat. (You can transfer the mixture to a bowl if you need to use the skillet for frying the quesadillas.)

Heat a 12-inch skillet over moderately high heat. Add 2 teaspoons vegetable oil. When oil is hot, place a tortilla in skillet. Sprinkle half the surface with one-fourth of the cheese, keeping the cheese away from the edge so it doesn't melt in the pan. Top cheese with one-fourth of the squash blossom mixture. Fold the untopped half over the filling, pressing gently. Move quesadilla into the center of the skillet and cook until bottom is browned in spots, about 3 minutes. Carefully turn with a metal spatula and cook until other side is nicely browned, about 3 minutes. Transfer to a cutting board, cut into wedges and serve on a warm plate with salsa. Repeat with remaining ingredients, making 4 quesadillas in all.

To make the salsa cruda: While quesadillas are cooking, combine all ingredients in a bowl, using as much of the jalapeño as you like.

Serve quesadillas with salsa on the side.

spaghettini with red and gold cherry tomatoes

Even in the hottest weather, I can muster an appetite for pasta dishes such as this one, made with olive oil, shallots, basil and the best barely cooked (or sometimes uncooked) tomatoes from the farmers' market. It is as sweet, natural and pure tasting as a sun-warmed sliced tomato on toast. Of course, the sauce would be just as tasty made with red tomatoes alone, but the gold tomatoes add eye appeal.

¾ POUND SMALL RED CHERRY TOMATOES SUCH AS SWEET 100, HALVED

¾ POUND SMALL GOLDEN CHERRY TOMATOES SUCH AS SUNGOLD, HALVED

3 LARGE SHALLOTS, MINCED

¼ CUP EXTRA VIRGIN OLIVE OIL

SCANT ¼ TEASPOON HOT RED PEPPER FLAKES

SALT AND FRESHLY GROUND BLACK PEPPER

1 POUND DRIED SPAGHETTINI

½ CUP LOOSELY PACKED FRESH BASIL LEAVES

SERVES 4 TO 6

In a large saute pan, combine tomatoes, shallots, olive oil, hot pepper flakes, and salt and black pepper to taste. Bring to a simmer over moderate heat and simmer until tomatoes render their juices, about 5 minutes. Remove from heat before the tomatoes completely collapse and lose their shape.

Bring a large pot of salted water to a boil over high heat. Add pasta and cook until al dente. Just before pasta is done, reheat sauce gently. Stack the basil leaves a few at a time and slice them into fine ribbons; add to sauce. Taste and adjust seasoning. Drain pasta and return it to pot. Add contents of skillet and toss well. Serve on warm plates.

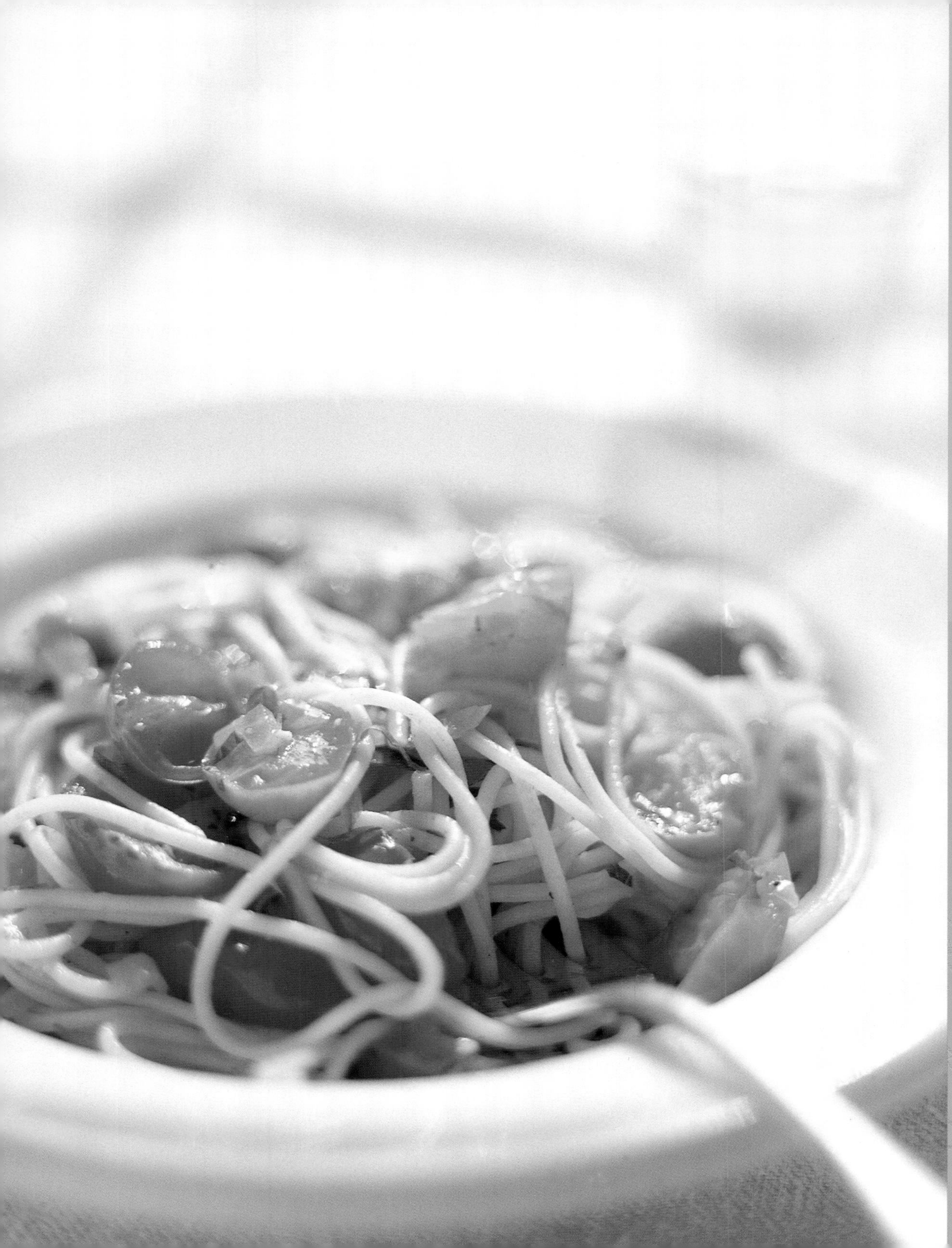

tomato salad with corn and basil

Made with tomatoes in a variety of sizes and colors, this photogenic salad is the essence of summer. At the farmers' market, look for small golden cherry tomatoes such as Sungold, green-when-ripe tomatoes such as Green Zebra, tiny Sweet 100 cherry tomatoes, bright red Early Girl tomatoes or the golden orange Mandarin Cross tomatoes. My version is inspired by a salad I had at Berkeley, California's Chez Panisse Cafe, where the season's best produce is always showcased in simple but irresistible ways.

3 TABLESPOONS EXTRA VIRGIN OLIVE OIL

1 TABLESPOON WHITE WINE VINEGAR

1 SHALLOT, MINCED

SALT AND PEPPER

1 POUND MIXED TOMATOES, IN DIFFERENT COLORS AND DIFFERENT SIZES

½ CUP CORN KERNELS

1 DOZEN FRESH BASIL LEAVES

SERVES 4

In a small bowl, whisk together olive oil, wine vinegar and shallot. Season highly with salt and pepper. Set aside for 15 minutes for flavors to blend.

Core large tomatoes. Halve through the stem end, lay cut side down and slice thinly. Halve cherry tomatoes. Arrange tomatoes attractively on a large serving platter, interspersing the different colors and putting the cherry tomatoes on top. Sprinkle corn kernels over the tomatoes. Tear basil leaves in small pieces and scatter over all. Spoon dressing evenly over the salad.

grand aioli

A platter of colorful boiled vegetables with aioli (garlic mayonnaise) is always appetizing to me, but when the vegetables come from the summer farmers' market, the presentation can be captivating. The recipe below is just a guide: your platter should vary with what you find at your market. Aim for a variety of colors and shapes, and take advantage of unusual varieties some growers may have, such as golden beets and fingerling potatoes. A grand aioli is an opportunity to show off the summer market's best, served with crusty bread, white wine and golden garlicky mayonnaise. Offer the dramatic still life as a first course; to make it a main course, add some boiled shrimp or poached salmon to the composition, or set out a separate platter of rosemary-scented grilled lamb.

The artichoke stands I refer to in the recipe can be ordered from Spanek, Inc., 800-446-3060.

1 POUND SMALL BEETS, PREFERABLY A MIX OF RED AND GOLD VARIETIES

6 SMALL LEEKS

1 DOZEN SMALL TURNIPS

½ POUND GREEN FILET BEANS (HARICOTS VERTS)

2 MEDIUM ARTICHOKES, TRIMMED (SEE NOTE)

1 POUND MIXED SMALL SUMMER SQUASHES SUCH AS GREEN AND GOLD PATTYPAN, GOLDEN ZUCCHINI AND GREEN RONDE DE NICE (ROUND ZUCCHINI)

1 POUND FINGERLING POTATOES OR OTHER WAXY NEW POTATOES

3 LARGE EGGS

FOR THE AIOLI:

3 LARGE CLOVES GARLIC

SALT

YOLKS FROM 3 LARGE EGGS

1 CUP OLIVE OIL

½ CUP EXTRA VIRGIN OLIVE OIL

FRESH LEMON JUICE

2 LARGE TOMATOES, PREFERABLY 1 RED AND 1 GOLD, IN THICK WEDGES

NIÇOISE OLIVES, FOR GARNISH

SERVES 8

Preheat oven to 375 degrees F. If beet greens are attached, remove all but ½ inch of the stems (so as not to pierce the beet) and reserve for another use. Put beets in a baking dish with ¼ cup water. Cover tightly and bake until a small knife slips in easily, about 45 minutes. Cool slightly, then peel. Keep red beets separate from yellow beets to preserve their colors.

Trim the leeks, removing the hairy roots without cutting into the base. Slit each leek partway, then wash under cold running water to remove dirt that may be trapped between the layers. If the turnips are small and thin skinned, there is no need to peel them; if they are not small, peel them. Trim the filet beans. Trim the artichokes (see note).

Bring 2 large pots of salted water to a boil. (Using 2 pots saves time.) Use these pots to boil the leeks, squashes, turnips, potatoes and filet beans. Boil each vegetable separately, removing it to a dish towel to drain as soon as it is just done. (Remember that they will continue to cook as they cool.) You do not have to change the water between vegetables; just lift each vegetable out with tongs or a slotted spoon and reuse the boiling water.

(CONTINUED)

NOTE: TO TRIM ARTICHOKES, FILL A MEDIUM BOWL WITH COLD WATER AND ADD THE JUICE OF ½ LEMON. CUT OFF AND DISCARD ALL BUT 1 INCH OF THE ARTICHOKE STEM. RUB THE CUT END OF THE STEM WITH A CUT LEMON. PEEL BACK AND DISCARD THE TINY TOUGH LEAVES AROUND THE BASE. WITH A SERRATED KNIFE, CUT ACROSS THE TOP OF THE ARTI-CHOKE TO REMOVE THE TOP QUARTER OR THIRD. RUB CUT SURFACE WITH CUT LEMON. WITH SCISSORS, SNIP ACROSS EACH EXPOSED OUTER LEAF TO REMOVE THE POINTED TIP. AS EACH ARTICHOKE IS TRIMMED, DROP IT INTO LEMON WATER TO PREVENT BROWNING UNTIL YOU ARE READY TO COOK THEM.

Cook the artichokes in a separate pot. I prefer to steam them upside down on artichoke stands over a small amount of boiling salted water, but you can also boil them in a large amount of salted water. Cook until the bottom is easily pierced with a knife. Drain upside down on a dish towel. When cool, quarter and scrape out the hairy choke.

Put eggs in a small saucepan with cold water to cover by 1 inch. Bring to a boil and remove from heat. Let stand 8 minutes, then drain and run under cold water until cool. Peel eggs. Set aside.

To make the aioli: In a mortar, pound garlic to a paste with a large pinch of salt. In a bowl, whisk egg yolks well, then begin adding oil drop by drop, whisking constantly, as for mayonnaise. When sauce thickens and clearly forms an emulsion, you can add the oil faster. When you have whisked in all the oil, whisk in the garlic. Season to taste with salt and lemon juice.

To serve, cut the beets and turnips in halves, quarters or thick wedges, depending on size. Cut round zucchini in wedges, long zucchini in thick rounds. Cut each leek in half lengthwise. Cut potatoes in halves or in large chunks. Quarter eggs. Arrange all the cooked vegetables, including artichokes and beans, the tomatoes and the eggs attractively on a serving platter. Scatter olives over all. Serve with aioli.

summer tomato soup with corn, hominy and okra

Southern cooks have dozens of ways to put corn, okra, tomatoes and green peppers together successfully. Here is another—a brothy soup that takes a Mexican turn with the addition of cilantro, oregano, chiles and hominy. Serve with hot tortillas and a green salad for a light dinner, or as a first course, followed by grilled pork with tortillas, guacamole and a jicama or zucchini salad.

4 THICK SLICES BACON, SLICED CROSSWISE IN ¼-INCH-WIDE STRIPS

1 SMALL ONION, CHOPPED

1 GREEN BELL PEPPER, SEEDS AND RIBS REMOVED, DICED

2 CLOVES GARLIC, MINCED

1 JALAPEÑO CHILE, SEEDS AND RIBS REMOVED, MINCED

½ TEASPOON DRIED MEXICAN OREGANO

½ POUND PLUM TOMATOES, PEELED, SEEDED AND FINELY DICED

6 CUPS HOMEMADE CHICKEN BROTH, OR 3 CUPS CANNED LOW-SODIUM CHICKEN BROTH AND 3 CUPS WATER

⅓ POUND OKRA, STEM ENDS REMOVED, CUT CROSSWISE IN ⅓-INCH-WIDE SLICES

2 CUPS CORN KERNELS

1½ CUPS COOKED HOMINY, RINSED IF CANNED

2 TABLESPOONS CHOPPED CILANTRO

SALT AND FRESHLY GROUND BLACK PEPPER

SERVES 4 TO 6

Cook bacon in a large, heavy pot over moderately low heat until it renders some of its fat, about 3 minutes. Add onion, bell pepper, garlic and jalapeño and saute until soft, about 15 minutes. Add oregano, crumbling it between your fingers to release its fragrance. Stir in tomatoes and saute over moderately high heat for 5 minutes, stirring often. Add broth and bring to a simmer. Simmer 5 minutes, uncovered. Add okra and cook at a gentle simmer until it is almost tender, about 15 minutes. Stir as little as possible to avoid releasing the sticky okra juices.

Stir in corn, hominy and cilantro. Cook, uncovered, at a gentle simmer until corn is done, about 10 minutes. Season with salt and a good deal of pepper and serve.

summer fruit compote with lemon verbena

If only for the fresh-cut citrus scent that's released when you brush up against it, it's worth growing lemon verbena. In one season, a four-inch pot will become a five-foot shrub that you can prune into a graceful tree shape. The narrow, pointed leaves are about two inches long and so fragrant that you don't need to crush or bruise them to release the aroma. In summer, when the plant puts out delicate white flowers, the branches are handsome in flower arrangements.

Pouring a hot wine syrup over lemon verbena leaves extracts their seductive fragrance. Then you can chill the syrup and spoon it over ripe summer fruit. At the farmers' market, look for fruit at peak ripeness: figs that have that drop of sweet nectar at the flower end and nectarines and berries that smell wonderful. As for wine, I would use a delicate white such as a Chenin Blanc, Riesling or Gewürztraminer. Some Chardonnays may be too oaky, some Sauvignon Blancs too grassy or tart.

1 CUP DRY WHITE WINE (SEE RECIPE INTRODUCTION)

⅓ CUP SUGAR

12 TO 16 FRESH LEMON VERBENA LEAVES

1 LARGE NECTARINE, PITTED AND SLICED

4 LARGE FRESH GREEN FIGS, QUARTERED

HALF A BOX (½ CUP) RASPBERRIES

HALF A BOX (½ CUP) BLACKBERRIES

SERVES 4

Combine wine, sugar and 1 cup water in a small pot. Bring to a simmer over moderately high heat, stirring to dissolve sugar. Simmer until reduced to 1 cup. Put 12 verbena leaves in a bowl and pour the syrup over them. Stir, let steep 5 minutes, then taste. Add a few more lemon verbena leaves if syrup doesn't seem flavorful enough. Cool to room temperature, then refrigerate until cold.

Divide the fruit evenly among 4 balloon wineglasses. Just before serving, strain the wine syrup to remove the lemon verbena leaves, then pour ¼ cup syrup over each portion of fruit. Alternatively, put all the fruit in a glass compote and pour all the syrup over it. Serve immediately.

MOESSNER
ORCHARDS
Tehachapi, CA 93561

APPLE MINT JELLY

Ingredients: Apple Cider, Sugar,
mint, and pectin.
Net wt. 8 fl ozs.

THE MARKET IN

autumn

The height of summer may seem like nature's most bountiful moment. But, in fact, as the days grow shorter and cooler, many fruits and vegetables mature—they fill out, develop sweetness, change color. Some—the sweet peppers and early apples and pears, for example—straddle the seasons, their harvest beginning in the heat of Indian summer but peaking in fall. By mid- to late season, the autumn market presents a palette of colors that mimics the changing leaves, with burgundy pomegranates, forest green squashes, russeted pears and pumpkin-colored persimmons.

Flat bean pods color and swell in late summer's long days. By early autumn, they are ready for shelling, yielding plump cranberry beans for vegetable soup and pasta, black-eyed peas for braising with spicy andouille sausage, or creamy Italian borlotto beans to season with olive oil, chopped onion and parsley.

Broccoli planted in mid-summer reaches perfection in fall; the tight florets, cooked and pureed with pine nuts and olive oil, make a verdant pasta sauce. Tender arugula also tempts autumn shoppers who enjoy its nutty taste in salads, with pasta or as a pizza topping. At some farmers' booths, customers inspect pale green fennel, its feathery leaves swaying, and imagine green salads or mushroom salads enhanced with the clean, cool taste of the sliced bulb. When frost threatens, growers bring their last unripe tomatoes to market—some of the fruits firm and green, others just barely blushing. The green ones can be floured and fried or chopped and sauteed with olive oil, garlic, pine nuts and basil for a pasta sauce. The others, left at room temperature, will gradually redden and soften; I've come to enjoy them in this slightly underripe state as Italians do, cut into wedges and added to a green salad.

In late autumn, shoppers survey the market with the Thanksgiving table in mind. They snap up the decorative hard-shelled squashes for centerpieces, soup and pies. Menus take shape around the available produce and new possibilities for the traditional dinner unfold—perhaps a sweet potato and chestnut soup, brussels sprouts in walnut oil, an apple and dried cherry crisp.

For those who seek more variety in daily meals, the autumn market obliges with fruits and vegetables that aren't yet commonplace on many tables. Asian pears, crisp and juicy, can be paired with prosciutto or sliced for dessert. Radicchio, an Italian chicory, can be braised with pine nuts and raisins or offered as a salad with celery heart and anchovies.

Fuyu and Hachiya persimmons, superb eating on their own, present numerous alternatives: the firm Fuyu can be sliced into green salads or combined in a fruit salad with pears and grapes; a frozen Hachiya, whipped with buttermilk or cream, makes a satisfying approximation of ice cream. The farmers' market, a direct route from farm to consumer, allows shoppers to taste this autumn produce at its best.

apples

With the exception of a few varieties that improve with storage, a tree-ripened apple eaten shortly after harvest is as good as an apple can get. Even the ubiquitous Red Delicious lives up to its name when it's right off the tree. But in storage, many apples lose their crisp snap and their sweet, juicy flavor.

To enjoy apples at their finest, it pays to shop at a farmers' market in early autumn and sample some of the more unusual varieties on offer. "There's a renaissance going on with antique apple varieties," says Stan Devoto, who grows 40 to 50 different apples at his Sebastopol, California, farm. Although they excel in flavor, many of these old-fashioned varieties have been ignored by large-scale commercial growers because they don't ship or store well or because their appearance doesn't meet with consumers' idea of perfection.

Don't look for Black Twig or Kidd's Orange Red at your neighborhood supermarket. Chances are the produce manager can't spare the space and needs greater quantities than these small growers can provide. But at the farmers' market, it doesn't matter that a grower only has a single case of Arkansas Black or Pink Pearl apples this week and that next week he may have none. Farmers' market shoppers don't demand to have the same apples week after week; they look forward to spotting and sampling the unfamiliar.

Devoto's favorite apples, naturally, are ones that do well in his Northern California climate. In other parts of the country, shoppers may find many other kinds. Sample varieties you don't know and take home some you haven't bought before. Growers can point you to the best varieties for pies, sauce, baking whole or eating out of hand.

selection: Some varieties have a seductive perfume, but many don't. The best way to find good apples is to ask for a taste.

Among Devoto's favorite apples for eating out of hand:

GRAVENSTEIN "The best eating and baking apple grown," says the grower. Unfortunately, this early-season apple is a poor keeper.

JONATHAN An excellent eating apple that is also great for apple butter, pies and cider.

FUJI This crisp apple has become enormously popular in a short time. When tree-ripened, it's splendid.

MUTSU A crisp, slightly tart apple with superb flavor; also good for pies.

BLACK TWIG "An incredible eating apple," says Devoto.

ARKANSAS BLACK A good storage apple; not as good right off the tree.

HAWAIIAN This sweet apple has a tropical fruit aftertaste, but it bruises too easily to interest most commercial growers.

SPITZENBURG Ben Franklin's favorite apple.

The grower also recommends Gravenstein, Mutsu, Spitzenburg and pippin for pies; Rome Beauty for baking; and Gravenstein, Mutsu, Jonathan and pippin for applesauce.

storage: "I think people should buy what they can consume in a week, or before the next market," says Devoto. Refrigerate to slow their breakdown.

arugula

The deep green, nutty arugula that American growers bring to farmers' markets today is an adaptation of a wild green that grows profusely in southern Italy and France. When young, the notched leaves have a pleasantly nutty flavor; as they get older and larger, they can become peppery and strong.

In the summer heat, arugula grows rapidly and growers have to work hard to keep it harvested young. In the cooler and shorter days of fall, it develops more slowly; the leaves get thicker and have better shelf life and flavor, says Northern California grower Andy Griffin.

Griffin grows baby arugula, the tender leaves picked at 30 to 45 days after their first irrigation, then washed and spun dry in an industrial salad spinner. They are sold by the pound at farmers' markets. You may also find older, sturdier arugula sold in bunches.

selection: Arugula should look perky and deep green; avoid limp bunches or those with yellowing leaves. For salads or uncooked dishes, choose young, nutty arugula. The spicy, older arugula is fine for cooked dishes.

storage: Supermarkets ruin arugula when they mist it, says Griffin. Arugula should not stay wet, because moisture causes the leaves to break down. If you buy arugula that has not already been washed and dried, when you get home wash it in a sinkful of cold water, spin it dry, then refrigerate it in a plastic bag with a paper towel to absorb any moisture. If kept dry, it should last several days.

asian pears

A good Asian pear has the crisp crunch of a new apple, the juiciness of a peach and the fragrance and taste of honey. From mid-August to Thanksgiving, these pears appear at farmers' markets and seduce all who sample them.

Sometimes called apple pears because of their crisp texture, they are botanically pears, not apples. You may find several different named varieties at farmers' markets—some, known as russets, with rough, golden brown skin; others with a smooth, yellow-green skin. Growers should be willing to offer samples so you can decide which variety you like best. The pears can vary considerably in sweetness, perfume and level of crunchiness depending on the variety, the growing climate and the degree to which they ripened on the tree.

In general, says Ted Richardson, a California grower, the russeted pears tend to be sweeter and more perfumed; the yellow-green types tend to be milder. Up to a point, says Richardson, the longer they stay on the tree, the better, as they develop a lot of their sugar in the last few days of ripening. But there is a subtle trade-off between sugar and crunch.

selection: At the farmers' market, look for Asian pears with full color. The russet types should be golden brown or orangish; the yellow-green ones should be more yellow than green. There are some greenish varieties such as 20th Century (which is also one of the juiciest), but in general, a green-tinged Asian pear will taste bland and ordinary. An appealing perfume also signals a delicious pear.

storage: Asian pears will keep for a few weeks in the refrigerator.

beans for shelling

"There is just no comparison," says grower Denesse Willey, speaking of the relative merits of dried beans and the fresh shelling beans she grows for farmers' markets. A dried bean is starchy; a fresh bean is creamy and sweet. A dried bean may take 90 minutes to cook; a fresh bean can take half that or much less. Unfortunately, many people believe they are too busy to shell fresh cranberry beans or black-eyed peas. They are missing a treat.

Fresh shelling beans are the halfway point between the flat green pod with unformed beans and the dry, papery pod with fully formed, dried beans. If left on the plant, fresh shelling beans would continue to dry out to yield the dried beans most people know. But harvest them a few weeks earlier, when the beans have formed but are still moist, and you will taste them at their best. You are unlikely to find them in this state at the supermarket, since they are highly perishable and not much in demand. But in early fall, growers bring them to farmers' markets where they know they have an eager audience.

"Probably our most loyal customers are our southern pea customers," says Willey. For people from the South, Willey's crowder peas (also known as cowpeas) and purple-hull peas are reminders of home. "People buy them by the crate," says the grower. "It's a big family thing. Everybody sits around and shells out peas."

The farmers' market is also the place to find fresh heirloom shelling beans such as French green flageolets, the striped Christmas limas, speckled cranberry beans or meaty Italian borlotto beans. Their rich taste and melting texture deliver an eating experience that dried beans can't duplicate.

selection: The pod should be leathery, says Willey, not crisp like a snap bean. You should be able to feel the fully formed beans inside. If the pod is dry and papery, however, the beans are at least partially dried. Because fresh beans are moist, they can mildew quickly. Watch for any sign of mold on the pod.

storage: Shell fresh beans as soon as you get home. Don't leave them in a plastic bag or they may mildew, says California grower Marcia Muzzi. If you aren't going to cook them that day or the next, Muzzi recommends freezing them.

broccoli

No matter how much produce I already have in my bags, I have a hard time passing a broccoli display at the farmers' market. Growers pile the stalks in high green hills, with their tempting blue-green floret faces pointing out. The florets look full and tight and the stalks have a bright, almost shiny appearance that supermarket broccoli rarely has. I can tell the broccoli isn't long off the plant and will be sweet and mild.

"Broccoli is like corn that way," says California grower Dru Rivers. The sooner you eat it after harvest, the sweeter it will be. At the market, it's a good idea to ask when the broccoli was picked, says Rivers.

Fall is probably the best season for most broccoli growers. They plant in late summer and the broccoli matures in the cooler weather it likes. Some growers in mild-winter areas plant in the fall for a spring crop, and some cool areas even bring in a summer crop. In addition to the familiar green heading broccoli, you may find purple sprouting broccoli, which, as its name indicates, forms small, tender flowering shoots. Also watch for broccoli romanesco, which looks like something Martians might grow. This heirloom variety forms a tight spiral of lime green, cone-shaped florets; the taste is somewhere between broccoli and cauliflower.

selection: Look for broccoli with slender, turgid stalks and a nice tight head with no yellowing. The butt end should be moist, not dry and cracked or hollow. Rivers says she sometimes forgoes the main head in favor of the slender side shoots that grow after the main head is harvested. They are so tender, they don't need peeling. Broccoli should smell sweet and mild, not strong and cabbagey.

storage: Refrigerate broccoli in an open plastic bag as soon as possible after purchase.

brussels sprouts

In early November, at the markets I frequent, shoppers' canvas totes start to look like dangerous weapons. Thick, sturdy green stalks poke out of them, ready to jab an adjacent shopper in the ribs. For brussels sprout fans like myself, the sight of these massive stalks, with the sprouts still clinging to them, suggests that there is no time to waste: the sprouts are freshly harvested and at their best.

More people would probably like brussels sprouts if they bought them at farmers' markets, where they are likely to be only a day or two off the plant. Their natural sweetness quickly disappears, and the flavor gets stronger the longer they are in refrigerated storage. (They stay sweeter if they are left on the stalk after harvest, as they continue to feed on it.) Packers can make older sprouts look deceptively fresh by washing them in acidulated water to keep the butts white, but they can't do anything about the deteriorating flavor.

selection: Buy brussels sprouts on the stalk if possible, and cook them as soon as you can. If you are buying loose sprouts, avoid any with yellow leaves or brown butts, both signs of age. Smaller ones tend to be milder, but freshness is even more important. Ask the grower when the sprouts were harvested.

storage: If you buy sprouts on the stalk, keep them on the stalk—in the refrigerator or in a cool garage—until you use them. Loose sprouts should be refrigerated in a plastic bag and cooked soon.

fennel

Growers tell me that fennel is not a big market seller unless there are Italians around. But perhaps with the growing interest in the healthful diet of Mediterranean peoples, interest in fennel will grow, too. Italians aren't the only ones who love it. French cooks pair fresh fennel with fish and chicken, grill seafood over the aromatic stalks, slice and marinate the bulb for a salad or bake it in a creamy gratin.

Also called anise, Florence fennel or bulb fennel (to distinguish it from varieties grown for their leaves and seeds), the vegetable prefers cool weather. The bulb—which is not botanically a bulb but a swollen base—grows above ground, and some farmers keep it white and tender by piling dirt around it. Thick celerylike stalks rise from the bulb and sport feathery leaves that look like fresh dill. The leaves and stalks are good for flavoring, but the bulb is the prize: crisp when raw, it has a pronounced licorice flavor that is muted when the bulb is cooked. The flavor is most pungent and the texture best when the bulb is freshly harvested and the stalks are attached, which is probably how you will find it at the farmers' market. Supermarket produce managers usually cut off the stalks and leaves when they no longer look fresh, which causes the bulb to dry out faster.

selection: Fennel should feel firm and solid and like it has a lot of moisture, says California grower Kachi Takahashi. Sometimes the outer layer is thick and fibrous or pithy and you have to discard it, so it's smarter to buy bulbs that have a smooth, nonfibrous outer layer.

storage: Store fennel in a plastic bag in the refrigerator. If you plan to use it within a day or two, leave the stalks attached. Otherwise, remove them to prevent decay.

green tomatoes

As any gardener knows, some tomatoes don't finish the race. Before they can ripen and redden, or turn whatever their final color may be, stragglers can be laid low by a freeze. To cut their losses, growers will harvest the hard green tomatoes ahead of the cold weather, hoping to find a home for them at the farmers' market. Fans of green tomatoes take advantage of their firmness and tart flavor in many dishes.

selection: For pickling and frying, choose green tomatoes that are fully green, with no hint of pink. For pies and pasta sauces, you can use tomatoes that are starting to color. These hard tomatoes won't have much aroma; just make sure they have no soft spots or serious blemishes.

storage: Store green tomatoes at cool room temperature, not by a sunny window. If you have a green-tomato recipe in mind, use them quickly, as they will start to soften and change color in just a few days.

hard-shelled squashes

You know the seasons are turning when the hot red, yellow and green of the summer farmers' market give way to the burnished gold and forest green of the autumn squash harvest.

With each passing week, the squash offerings become more fantastic, with striped green-and-white Sweet Dumplings and bumpy Blue Hubbards heaped next to smooth, shapely Butternuts and decorative mini pumpkins, both orange and white.

If you appreciate choice and enjoy discovery, shop for autumn squashes at the farmers' market. Growers there are more willing to try unfamiliar varieties that take some hand-selling. They can tell you firsthand about a squash's features and weaknesses, how it cooks and how it tastes.

Harvested in autumn, these hard-shelled squashes are often referred to as winter squashes because they can be stored for weeks or months under the proper conditions. Their fabulous autumn colors and shapes are a pleasing sight on a kitchen countertop and make a holiday table look properly festive. My favorites are the Kabocha, a Japanese squash with dense, sweet, deep orange flesh like a moist sweet potato's, and the Butternut, which has a small seed cavity, is easy to peel and has a high proportion of usable, sweet, dense orange meat.

selection: Trust growers to point you to the squash variety that's best for the dish you are making. Of course, squash should not have any soft spots. Look for a dull rind; a sheen indicates lack of maturity. With the buff-colored Butternut, greenish streaks on the skin are a sign that it's underripe. If you are making a recipe that calls for peeling raw squash, try to select a squash that's relatively easy to peel, such as Butternut or Kabocha. Otherwise, you may need to cut up the squash and steam wedges slightly first to help release the flesh from the peel.

storage: Store hard-shelled squashes in a cool, dark, well-ventilated place. Once you cut into a squash, wrap and refrigerate any unused portion.

pears

Even at a farmers' market, you won't find growers boasting about their tree-ripened pears. Rare among fruits, pears ripen best when picked hard and green and allowed to sweeten and soften off the tree. A pear left on the tree until it is sweet will be mushy and unpleasant.

Still, a grower can't harvest too early or the pear will never ripen properly. It must hang on the tree long enough to fill with the starches that will convert to sugar during ripening. Typically, fresh-picked pears go immediately into cold storage where they can stay, depending on the variety, for months. Brought to room temperature as needed, they will complete their ripening in anywhere from a few days to two weeks.

Al Courchesne, a California grower, says consumers should not come to the market expecting to find pears for eating that evening or the next day. Instead, plan your purchases one to two weeks ahead of your need.

At the farmers' market, farmers like Courchesne try to educate consumers about how to ripen pears and how to judge readiness. Courchesne typically brings some ripe pears for sampling, so buyers know what they should aim for. The unfortunate grocery store customer, in contrast, often simply rejects pears as too hard and green. Those who buy them often let them get too soft and then discover they are mealy inside.

As farmers' market shoppers learn, good pears are worth waiting for. Creamy-textured, juicy and sweet, they are one of nature's most satisfying desserts.

selection: Green-skinned Anjous, golden Bartletts and russeted, slender-necked Boscs are among the more familiar pear varieties you will find at a farmers' market. But keep your eye out for more unusual types, such as the luscious Comice, a plump, neckless pear that turns from green to gold as it ripens; the russet-skinned Winter Nelis, with its sweet, winey flesh; the ravishing Red Bartlett, similar in taste to the golden Bartlett but with a full red blush; and the exquisite, velvety French Butter pear.

storage: Store unripe pears at room temperature on a counter or in a fruit bowl. To hasten the ripening, put them in a closed paper bag with a banana or an apple. These fruits give off ethylene gas that will make the pears ripen faster. You will know your pears are ripe when they give slightly to pressure at the stem end. Don't wait until the whole fruit is soft or you will have a mealy pear. Once ripe, pears can be refrigerated for a few days.

persimmons

At the San Francisco Bay Area farmers' markets with a large Chinese clientele—such as Oakland's downtown market or San Francisco's Alemany market—you can tell the Fuyu persimmon stalls by the clusters of shoppers. Firm when ripe, the squat, round Fuyus are crisp, virtually seedless and almost candy-sweet, perfect additions to green salads with red onions or walnuts or an arugula salad with pears. When vendors offer me a Fuyu sample, they make a sale.

Hachiya persimmons, the large, heart-shaped variety, are not ready to eat until they are squishy soft. At that point, they have a puddinglike texture and a satisfying sweetness and can be used for puddings or quick breads, or simply halved and drizzled with cream. Underripe ones, in contrast, are full of mouth-puckering tannins; take a bite and that persimmon may be your last.

Because they can take a long time to ripen and are so fragile when ripe, few supermarkets want to handle Hachiyas. At a farmers' market, a grower can take the time to explain to shoppers how to properly ripen firm Hachiyas at home.

selection: A good Fuyu will be firm, not hard, and a deep orange-red. If its leafy cap is dry and brittle, it was not freshly picked. Generally, the Fuyus harvested early in the season are not as sweet as those harvested later, around Thanksgiving. Hachiya persimmons should have good orange color from tip to stem end. You can buy them at the firm or soft stage, depending on how soon you intend to eat them. A firm Hachiya may take two weeks or more to soften completely.

storage: Keep Fuyus at room temperature if you expect to eat them shortly; refrigerate them if you don't want them to soften further. Hachiyas should be kept at room temperature until completely soft, then refrigerated. Putting the fruit in a paper bag with an apple or banana will hasten ripening.

pomegranates

This age-old fruit, celebrated in Greek mythology, in the Bible, in poetry and in art, has a rich history as a fertility symbol. Split open, its vivid red seeds spill out, a sight that suggested to the ancients that the fruit might pass its reproductive properties on to those who ate it.

Whether you want more children, or any children, the pomegranate is a fruit to look forward to. The juice is refreshingly sweet-tart, the jewellike seeds a sparkling garnish on salads and desserts.

Pomegranates don't make themselves easy to appreciate. The juice stains everything, so take precautions. To open, slice a thin piece off the crown end of the fruit to expose the seeds. With a knife, slit the skin from top to bottom in four equidistant places, taking care not to pierce the seed sacs. Then, holding the fruit in both hands, pull it open. You can eat the juicy seed sacs with a spoon, discarding the white membrane. If you don't like the crunchy seeds, try this method: Gently but firmly roll the fruit around on a hard surface to break the inner seeds sacs, taking care not to allow the skin to break. Then pierce the skin (watch out: juice will spurt) and insert a straw or squeeze out the juice.

selection: Most people want a perfect pomegranate with no cracking, so many farmers pick the fruit underripe, says California grower Ignacio Sanchez. At the farmers' market, look instead for pomegranates that have a few cracks, which indicate that the fruit is ripe and beginning to burst. They should feel heavy for their size, sign of plenty of juice inside.

storage: Pomegranates will keep for a month at room temperature, or refrigerate them if you like them cold.

radicchio

Italians write poetry about it, hold fairs around it and, in Treviso in December, devote a whole market to it. Prized by cooks, especially in the Veneto region, where most of it is grown, radicchio beautifies Italian markets from September through March. "The undisputed king of the winter table," one Italian writer calls it.

At last, radicchio is becoming more available in this country, spurred no doubt by the American passion for Italian food. And gradually, American farmers are discovering where radicchio performs best. This stunningly beautiful member of the chicory family prefers to mature in cool weather; in hot weather, it tends to turn bitter.

At the farmers' market, you are most likely to find heading radicchio—tight burgundy globes with white ribs and veins. But a few growers are also cultivating the elongated, romainelike type known as *radicchio di Treviso*, a variety that Italians consider superior.

selection: Heading radicchio should have some give. If it is too firm and heavy, with leaves no longer attached to the core, it is probably overmature and won't last long. With all types, select radicchio as you would any salad green, avoiding specimens that show signs of decay such as brown-edged leaves or browning cores.

storage: Store in a loose plastic bag in the refrigerator crisper. Radicchio keeps a few days longer than most salad greens.

sweet peppers

The luscious technicolor array of sweet peppers at the autumn farmers' market puts the grocery store display to shame. Thanks to plant breeders and seed savers, we have long, skinny Corno di Toro peppers shaped like the bull's horn they are named for; heart-shaped red pimientos and flattened globe pimientos; crunchy red cherry peppers and small green Italian peperoncini for pickling; chocolate-colored (but, regrettably, not chocolate-flavored) peppers; yellow, gold, orange, purple and even cream-colored peppers; and multihued peppers that look like the setting sun.

For California grower Christine Coke, there's no reason to eat a green pepper anymore. "A green pepper to me is not a ripe pepper," says Coke, and technically she's right. All peppers start out green, changing to their final ripe color as they mature. The green peppers you see at the market have been harvested before maturity, before they had a chance to develop sugar and change color. They will never be as sweet as a red or gold pepper, but their "greener" taste is desirable in some dishes.

By getting them to the farmers' market soon after harvest, growers try to make sure that you will get a crunchy, juicy pepper with its field moisture intact. Large-scale growers who sell to supermarkets sometimes wax their peppers to prevent moisture loss in the several days it takes the peppers to get to the shelves, says Coke.

selection: Peppers should feel crisp and firm and have glossy skins with no wrinkling. If you need them to be thick-walled—for stuffing or for roasting and peeling—look for peppers that feel heavy for their size. (Some of the specialty peppers are naturally thin-walled.) Moist, green stems also guide you to peppers that were freshly picked.

storage: You can keep peppers in a paper bag at cool room temperature if you will be using them in a day or two, but they last longer in the refrigerator. Protect from moisture loss by putting them in a paper bag or dry plastic bag in the crisper.

sweet potatoes

In nine cases out of ten, quality and freshness go hand in hand at the farmers' market. If you want the best-tasting fruits and vegetables, you buy the ones that were just picked or just dug.

Sweet potatoes are the tenth case. They not only need to cure after harvest to harden the skins, but the flavor also improves with storage. A fresh-dug sweet potato has a high proportion of starch to sugar. Given proper storage, the starch converts to sugar, producing the almost candylike sweetness that consumers expect.

Sweet potato growers divide varieties into two distinct camps: moist fleshed and dry fleshed. The moist types—such as Garnet, Centennial and Jewel—are what many people call yams. (They are not true yams, however.) They tend to have dense, waxy orange flesh that's moist and sweet. Dry-fleshed sweet potatoes, many with Japanese names such as Kintoki and Kotobuki, tend to have yellow meat that's fluffier, less sweet and with more of a chestnut taste.

Breeders are constantly trying to invent a better sweet potato, one that's more shapely and uniform, with fewer eyes and less tendency to mutate. Their most recent triumph is Beauregard, a copper-skinned, orange-fleshed moist sweet potato that growers praise for its good behavior and great taste.

Even after curing, growers have to handle thin-skinned sweet potatoes delicately and as little as possible to prevent further damage. "When we ship our sweet potatoes, they look beautiful," one California sweet potato marketer told me. "But by the time they get to retail stores, they've been handled many times on delivery trucks and in the warehouse. Sometimes I look at them and say, 'These are not my potatoes.' They're skinned up and bruised up. And if they sit there, the bruise spots will develop rot."

By shopping at a farmers' market, you improve the chances that the sweet potatoes you buy have gone through fewer channels and suffered less damage than their supermarket equivalents. You will probably also find a wider choice of sweet potato varieties and knowledgeable growers who can tell you about the cooking and eating qualities of each.

selection: Look for firm sweet potatoes with a smooth skin and no soft spots or sunken pits. Surface bruises that have sealed over with a whitish patch are not a problem, but avoid potatoes with black patches.

storage: Store sweet potatoes in a cool, dark, well-ventilated place. Never refrigerate them; they don't like cold.

apple and dried cherry crisp with crème fraîche ice cream

For the best results with this crisp, ask at the farmers' market for a sweet, juicy apple that's good when cooked. Gravensteins would be my first choice, but any apple grower should be able to point you to his or her best variety for pies and crisps. In other seasons, use the same crumb topping to make a peach or strawberry-rhubarb crisp.

Accompany this warm apple crisp (or any fruit pie or crisp) with a soft scoop of Crème Fraîche Ice Cream, a recipe based on one kindly given to me by Domaine Chandon chef Philippe Jeanty. Crème fraîche gives the ice cream a subtle sour-cream flavor reminiscent of cheesecake.

½ CUP PITTED DRIED SOUR OR SWEET CHERRIES

2 POUNDS APPLES (SEE RECIPE INTRODUCTION)

¼ CUP GRANULATED SUGAR

¾ CUP UNBLEACHED ALL-PURPOSE FLOUR

3 TABLESPOONS BROWN SUGAR

¼ TEASPOON GROUND CINNAMON

PINCH SALT

6 TABLESPOONS UNSALTED BUTTER, IN SMALL PIECES

⅓ CUP OLD-FASHIONED ROLLED OATS

½ CUP CHOPPED TOASTED WALNUTS

CRÈME FRAÎCHE ICE CREAM

1 CUP HALF-AND-HALF

1 CUP HEAVY CREAM

½ VANILLA BEAN, SPLIT LENGTH-WISE

¾ CUP SUGAR

YOLKS OF 6 LARGE EGGS

1 CUP CRÈME FRAÎCHE

MAKES 1 QUART

SERVES 6

Put cherries in a small bowl with just enough water to cover. Let stand 1 hour, then drain.

Preheat oven to 375 degrees F.

Quarter, core and peel the apples. Cut each quarter crosswise into ¼-inch-thick slices. In a large bowl, combine apple slices and 2 tablespoons granulated sugar. Toss to coat.

In electric mixer with the paddle attachment, combine flour, remaining 2 tablespoons granulated sugar, the brown sugar, cinnamon and salt. Mix on low until well blended. Add butter pieces and mix until mixture resembles coarse crumbs. Add oatmeal and walnuts and mix on medium-low until mixture forms clumps; it may take 2 or 3 minutes.

Layer apples in a 10-inch pie pan, sprinkling cherries evenly between the layers. Make sure no cherries are exposed or they will burn. Cover with topping, pressing it lightly into an even layer. Bake until topping is browned and filling is bubbly, about 55 minutes.

Crème Fraîche Ice Cream: Put half-and-half and cream in a saucepan. Scrape the seeds out of the vanilla pod into the cream mixture, then add the pod halves as well. Bring mixture to a simmer over moderate heat, remove from heat and let stand 15 minutes.

With a whisk, beat sugar and egg yolks until mixture is pale and forms a ribbon when whisk is lifted. Gradually beat in hot cream mixture. Return to saucepan and cook over moderately low heat, stirring constantly with a wooden spoon, until mixture visibly thickens, about 3 minutes. Do not let it boil or it will curdle. Cool 15 minutes, then add crème fraîche, whisking until smooth. Remove vanilla bean pods. Cover and chill mixture thoroughly. Freeze in an ice cream maker according to manufacturer's directions.

pizza with mozzarella and arugula

One evening in Rome, my husband and I decided to have dinner at a pizzeria in Trastevere that had been mentioned in a couple of guidebooks. But when we found it, I groaned: the place was almost empty, and the few diners inside looked like tourists. We closed the guidebook, kept on walking and soon came upon a much more appetizing sight: a brightly lit pizzeria with a wood-fired oven, a full house inside and at least 100 more people at sidewalk tables. We sat outside in Rome's mild night air and ate pizzas so light and thin that you could pick them up and roll them like a burrito. My favorite had nothing on it but cheese and a shower of fresh arugula.

It is probably impossible to re-create these Roman pizzas without a wood-burning oven, but allowing the dough a long, slow rise gives the best possible texture. One ounce of arugula may not seem like much, but it's enough; think of it as an herb that's scattered on top at the end.

FOR THE PIZZA DOUGH:

1½ TEASPOONS ACTIVE DRY YEAST

¾ CUP WARM WATER

1 TABLESPOON OLIVE OIL

1 TEASPOON SALT

APPROXIMATELY 1¾ CUPS UNBLEACHED ALL-PURPOSE FLOUR

FOR THE TOPPING:

2 TABLESPOONS EXTRA VIRGIN OLIVE OIL

1 LARGE GARLIC CLOVE, MINCED

¼ TEASPOON HOT RED PEPPER FLAKES

SALT

½ POUND LOW-MOISTURE WHOLE-MILK MOZZARELLA, COARSELY GRATED

1 OUNCE ARUGULA

CORNMEAL, FOR DUSTING

To make the dough: Sprinkle yeast over warm water in a large bowl and let stand 2 minutes. Stir with a fork to blend. Let stand until bubbly, about 10 minutes. Whisk in olive oil and salt. Add 1½ cups

(CONTINUED)

flour, stirring with a wooden spoon. Turn dough out onto a lightly floured board and knead until dough is smooth and elastic, 6 to 8 minutes, using as much of the remaining ¼ cup flour as needed to keep dough from sticking to the board or your hands. Shape into a ball, transfer to an oiled bowl, turn dough to coat with oil, then cover tightly with plastic wrap and let rise 2 hours.

Punch dough down, reshape into a ball, recover the bowl and let dough rise again for 4 hours.

Position a rack in the center of the oven. Line rack with baking tiles or a baking stone. Preheat to 550 degrees F or highest setting for at least 45 minutes. Punch dough down and turn it out onto a work surface. Shape into a ball. Cover with a clean dish towel and let rest 30 minutes.

To make the topping: In a small bowl, combine olive oil, garlic, hot-pepper flakes and salt to taste. Let stand 30 minutes to marry flavors.

To assemble pizza: On a lightly floured surface, roll out dough into a 13- to 14-inch round. Transfer to a pizza peel or rimless baking sheet well dusted with cornmeal. Working quickly, spread cheese evenly over the pizza dough, leaving a ¾-inch rim. (If you don't work quickly, the dough may stick to the peel or sheet.) Brush the rim with some of the seasoned oil, then drizzle more oil, including the garlic and pepper flakes, over the pizza. Reserve a little oil for brushing on the rim after baking.

Immediately slide pizza from peel onto oven tiles or stone and bake until crust is crisp and browned, about 8 minutes. Remove from oven. Scatter arugula over the top. Brush rim of crust with remaining olive oil. Serve immediately.

MAKES ONE 13- TO 14-INCH PIZZA, TO SERVE 2

asian pears with prosciutto and baby greens

Sweet, juicy Asian pears are exquisite with prosciutto, an autumn alternative to the more traditional melons or figs. I add baby greens to make a more substantial salad and use a vinaigrette with a little walnut oil to bring the parts together. At some farmers' markets you can find a salad mix with edible flowers, which makes this dish even prettier. The recipe makes about twice as much vinaigrette as you will need, but it keeps for several days in the refrigerator.

FOR THE VINAIGRETTE:

1 LARGE SHALLOT, MINCED

1 TABLESPOON CHAMPAGNE VIN-EGAR

1 TEASPOON DIJON MUSTARD

1 TABLESPOON WALNUT OIL

2 TABLESPOONS EXTRA VIRGIN OLIVE OIL

SALT AND FRESHLY GROUND BLACK PEPPER

8 THIN SLICES PROSCIUTTO DI PARMA

¼ POUND MIXED BABY GREENS

1 TABLESPOON CHOPPED ITALIAN PARSLEY OR CHERVIL

½ LARGE ASIAN PEAR (APPLE PEAR), HALVED AGAIN, CORED, PEELED AND SLICED INTO THIN WEDGES

SERVES 4

To make the vinaigrette: In a small bowl, whisk together shallot, vinegar and mustard. Gradually whisk in oils to make an emulsion. Season generously with salt and pepper. Taste and add a few drops more vinegar if necessary. Let stand 30 minutes to marry flavors.

Arrange 2 slices prosciutto on each of 4 dinner plates, covering each plate's surface. Toss greens and parsley or chervil with enough dressing just to coat them lightly, 2 to 3 tablespoons; taste and adjust seasoning. Divide the greens among the 4 plates, mounding them in the center. Nestle the Asian pear slices around the edge of each mound of greens.

cavatelli with cranberry beans

Almost any fresh shelling bean would work in this recipe, but the meaty cranberry beans are particularly satisfying and have the proper Italian taste. Look for the beans in their mottled red-and-cream pods at the farmers' market in late summer or early fall. They are easy to shell.

2 POUNDS FRESH UNSHELLED CRAN-
BERRY BEANS

5 LARGE CLOVES GARLIC

½ ONION

6 FRESH THYME SPRIGS

SALT AND FRESHLY GROUND
BLACK PEPPER

¼ CUP EXTRA VIRGIN OLIVE OIL,
PLUS MORE FOR GARNISH

2 TABLESPOONS CHOPPED ITALIAN
PARSLEY

1 TABLESPOON CHOPPED FRESH
SAGE

⅛ TEASPOON HOT RED PEPPER
FLAKES

½ POUND TOMATOES, PEELED,
SEEDED AND FINELY DICED

1 POUND DRIED CAVATELLI OR
GNOCCHI PASTA

SERVES 6

Like all beans, these taste best when they have a chance to rest for a day or so in their cooking medium. With this recipe, my preference is to make the beans two days ahead, then make the sauce one day ahead and let the beans rest in it overnight. You could offer grated Parmesan cheese with this dish, but I think a better choice is a bottle of extra virgin olive oil for anointing the beans at the table.

Shell cranberry beans; you should have about 3 cups. Put beans in a large pot. Lightly smack 2 garlic cloves and add to pot along with onion, thyme sprigs and 6 cups water. Bring to a simmer over moderately high heat, then partially cover, adjust heat to maintain a bare simmer and cook until beans are tender, begin checking at 30 minutes, but they may take an hour or more, depending on their age. When tender, season well with salt and pepper and let cool in broth. (You can cook the beans to this point a day or two ahead.)

Mince the remaining 3 garlic cloves. Heat ¼ cup olive oil in a 12-inch skillet over moderately low heat. Add parsley, sage, hot-pepper flakes and garlic. Cook a minute or two to soften the garlic and release its fragrance. Add the tomato and 1 cup of the bean-cooking liquid. Season with salt and pepper. Bring to a simmer, cover and adjust heat to maintain a simmer. Cook, covered, 20 minutes. Drain beans, reserving liquid. Discard the onion, garlic and thyme sprigs. Add beans to the skillet and simmer, uncovered, for 10 minutes to allow beans to absorb flavors. For best flavor, let the beans cool in the sauce at this point for a few hours or refrigerate overnight.

Bring a large pot of salted water to a boil over high heat. Add pasta and cook until al dente. While pasta is cooking, reheat beans, adding some or all of the reserved bean liquid if necessary; beans should be brothy. Drain pasta and return it to pot. Add beans and sauce. Toss well, then serve in warm bowls, drizzling each portion with additional olive oil.

black-eyed peas with andouille

It doesn't take much andouille—a spicy, smoky pork sausage—to make a pot of black-eyed peas so savory you can hardly stop eating them. The peas take a lot of seasoning, so be liberal with the salt and pepper. Make the dish a day ahead to allow the peas to absorb the flavors, then reheat and serve over steamed rice as a main course.

Don't deny yourself the pleasure of fresh black-eyed peas at the farmers' market because shelling them seems too tedious. Recruit a helper and take the beans outside so you can enjoy the sunshine and some conversation as you work.

If you can't find andouille locally, contact Aidells Sausage Company, 800-546-5795.

1½ POUNDS FRESH UNSHELLED BLACK-EYED PEAS OR PURPLE-HULLED PEAS

2 TABLESPOONS OLIVE OIL

1 LARGE GREEN BELL PEPPER, SEEDS AND RIBS REMOVED, DICED

1 LARGE ONION, MINCED

4 LARGE CLOVES GARLIC, MINCED

¾ POUND PLUM TOMATOES, PEELED, SEEDED AND FINELY DICED

SALT

1½ CUPS HOMEMADE OR CANNED LOW-SODIUM CHICKEN BROTH

3 OUNCES CAJUN-STYLE ANDOUILLE SAUSAGE, CHOPPED

1 BAY LEAF

2 TABLESPOONS MINCED ITALIAN PARSLEY

FRESHLY GROUND BLACK PEPPER

SERVES 6

Shell the peas; you should have about 3 cups. Bring 6 cups of water to a boil over high heat. Add peas and simmer gently until just tender, 12 to 15 minutes. (Do not overcook as they will continue to cook in the sauce.) Drain, reserving cooking liquid.

Heat olive oil in a large pot or 12-inch skillet over moderate heat. Add bell pepper, onion and garlic and saute until vegetables soften, about 15 minutes. Stir in tomatoes, season with salt and bring to a simmer. Cover, reduce heat to maintain a simmer and cook 15 minutes.

Stir in broth, 1½ cups of reserved bean-cooking liquid, andouille, bay leaf and parsley. Simmer 10 minutes. Season with salt and pepper. Add peas, cover, adjust heat to maintain a gentle simmer and cook 15 minutes. Remove from heat, remove bay leaf and let peas cool in sauce. For best flavor, refrigerate overnight; reheat to serve.

warm shelling beans with chopped onion, parsley and olive oil

I typically cook dried beans with a prosciutto bone or ham hock, but fresh beans seem to need more delicate treatment. To my taste, a light broth made with fresh pork ribs enhances the beans without masking their flavor. Serve them warm as a first course with olive oil, onions and parsley for diners to add to their taste. The cooked ribs should be reserved, marinated in olive oil with rosemary and garlic, then grilled or broiled until brown and crusty. Serve as a second course with some wilted spinach or chard.

This basic recipe can be made with whatever fresh shelling beans appear in your farmers' market. Try it with lima, cannellini, garbanzo, cranberry or borlotto beans, black-eyed or crowder peas, or a combination.

2 POUNDS BONE-IN PORK, SUCH AS SPARERIBS OR BABY BACK RIBS
1 ONION, HALVED
2 DOZEN BLACK PEPPERCORNS
2 BAY LEAVES
SALT

4 POUNDS SHELLING BEANS, ONE VARIETY OR SEVERAL (SEE RECIPE INTRODUCTION)

GARNISHES:
1 LARGE RED ONION, CHOPPED
1/3 CUP CHOPPED ITALIAN PARSLEY
2 TOMATOES, CHOPPED (OPTIONAL)
EXTRA VIRGIN OLIVE OIL
KOSHER SALT
FRESHLY GROUND BLACK PEPPER

SERVES 4

In a large pot, combine pork and 10 cups water. Bring to a simmer over moderate heat, skimming any foam that collects on the surface. Add halved onion, peppercorns and bay leaves. Adjust heat to maintain a simmer and cook until broth is rich tasting, about 1 hour. Season with salt. Cool, then strain. Discard the seasonings but reserve the ribs for grilling, if desired. Refrigerate broth overnight. The next day, skim off and discard the congealed fat on the surface.

Shell the beans, keeping the varieties separate. Cook each variety separately, bringing them to a simmer in a saucepan with enough of the broth to cover, then covering and simmering gently until tender. Cooking times will depend on the size and age of the beans. For example, fresh black-eyed peas cook quickly, in 12 to 15 minutes, while limas may take considerably longer. Add more hot broth or hot water if needed to keep the beans submerged in liquid. When done, cool slightly in liquid.

To serve, prepare the garnishes—onions, parsley and tomatoes (if using)—and put in separate bowls on the table. Set out olive oil, kosher salt and a pepper mill. Lift beans out of their cooking liquid with a slotted spoon. You can combine them in a serving bowl or serve each variety in a separate bowl if you prefer to savor their distinctive tastes. Diners should help themselves to beans and stir in garnishes as desired. I like mine with a great deal of chopped onion.

penne with broccoli sauce

This recipe calls for broccoli crowns—the tightly bunched, deep green florets with just about an inch of stem attached. If the broccoli you buy at the farmers' market has more stem, don't throw it away. Pare the stem down to its pale heart and enjoy it as a crisp, raw nibble, or dice and add to a salad. If you have leftover sauce, enjoy it the following day as a spread on warm toasts.

2 TABLESPOONS PINE NUTS

½ POUND BROCCOLI CROWNS (SEE RECIPE INTRODUCTION)

16 TO 18 FRESH BASIL LEAVES

1 GARLIC CLOVE, THINLY SLICED

6 TABLESPOONS EXTRA VIRGIN OLIVE OIL

2 TABLESPOONS HEAVY CREAM

6 TABLESPOONS FRESHLY GRATED PARMESAN CHEESE

SALT AND FRESHLY GROUND BLACK PEPPER

1 POUND DRIED PENNE OR FUSILLI

SERVES 4 TO 6

Preheat oven to 325 degrees F. Toast pine nuts on a baking sheet until they are golden brown and fragrant, 12 to 15 minutes. Cool.

Bring a large pot of salted water to a boil over high heat. Add broccoli and cook 3 minutes, then transfer with tongs to a sieve and drain well. Reserve the boiling water for cooking the pasta.

Cut broccoli into large chunks and place in food processor with basil and garlic. Process until finely chopped, stopping to scrape down sides of bowl once or twice. With motor running, add olive oil and cream through feed tube, processing until mixture is well blended and nearly smooth. Add pine nuts and process again until they are finely chopped. Transfer mixture to a bowl and stir in cheese and salt and pepper to taste.

Add pasta to the same boiling water used to cook the broccoli. Cook until al dente. Just before pasta is done, remove 1 cup of the boiling water. Whisk enough of the water into the broccoli mixture to make a sauce that will coat the pasta nicely.

Drain pasta and return it to pot. Add about two-thirds of the sauce and toss well. Add more sauce, if desired, and toss again. Serve on warm plates.

brussels sprouts with walnut oil

Farmers' markets may be the best thing ever to happen to brussels sprouts. I suspect many people have been inspired to cook them after seeing them at the market on their clublike stalks. Certainly, the sweet, mild taste of fresh-picked sprouts has made some converts. When I make them this way for Thanksgiving, they are the first vegetable to disappear.

1 TABLESPOON UNSALTED BUTTER

1 ½ TABLESPOONS WALNUT OIL

2 TABLESPOONS CHOPPED ITALIAN PARSLEY

2 TABLESPOONS THINLY SLICED FRESH CHIVES

1 POUND SMALL BRUSSELS SPROUTS

SALT AND FRESHLY GROUND BLACK PEPPER

SERVES 4

Put butter, walnut oil, parsley and chives in a serving bowl and set aside.

Trim brussels sprout ends. Bring a large pot of salted water to a boil over high heat. Add sprouts and cook until just tender, about 10 minutes. Drain and return to pot over low heat. Cook briefly, shaking the pot, until any water has evaporated.

Transfer sprouts to the serving bowl and season well with salt and pepper. Toss until butter melts and seasonings evenly coat the sprouts.

fennel and mushroom salad with mint

With its crisp, celerylike texture and subtle licorice flavor, fennel bulb inspires some inviting salads. Serve this one as a first course, perhaps with some boiled shrimp marinated in lemon, olive oil and the chopped feathery fennel leaves—a farmers' market bonus you don't always get at the grocery store. The salad is best when it is freshly dressed; you can slice the fennel and mushrooms an hour or two ahead, but add the vinaigrette just before serving.

1 LARGE FENNEL BULB

¾ POUND FRESH MUSHROOMS, HALVED IF LARGE, THEN THINLY SLICED

SCANT 2 TEASPOONS DIJON MUSTARD

2 TABLESPOONS WHITE WINE VINEGAR

1 LARGE SHALLOT, MINCED

¼ CUP EXTRA VIRGIN OLIVE OIL

SALT AND FRESHLY GROUND BLACK PEPPER

2 TABLESPOONS CHOPPED FRESH MINT

SERVES 4

Remove fennel stalks, if attached. Quarter the bulb lengthwise and cut away the core. Remove the outer layer if it is thick and fibrous. Slice the bulb crosswise as thinly as possible. Transfer to a bowl and add the sliced mushrooms.

In a small bowl, whisk together mustard, wine vinegar and shallot. Slowly whisk in olive oil to make a vinaigrette. Season with salt and pepper.

Add vinaigrette to salad along with mint. Toss well. Taste and adjust seasoning.

fennel and prosciutto gratin

Layers of sliced fennel, creamy béchamel sauce and crunchy bread crumbs make a luscious gratin. Serve with roast chicken or pork.

1 TABLESPOON OLIVE OIL

¾ CUP FINE BREAD CRUMBS (SEE NOTE, PAGE 41)

SALT

2 TABLESPOONS UNSALTED BUTTER, PLUS MORE FOR THE BAKING DISH

2½ TABLESPOONS ALL-PURPOSE FLOUR

1 CUP MILK, OR MORE IF NEEDED

1 CUP HOMEMADE OR CANNED LOW-SODIUM CHICKEN BROTH

1 BAY LEAF

2 FRESH THYME SPRIGS

1 GARLIC CLOVE, HALVED

FRESHLY GROUND BLACK PEPPER

1 POUND FENNEL BULBS (WEIGHT AFTER STALKS ARE REMOVED), ABOUT 2 MEDIUM BULBS

1 OUNCE THINLY SLICED PROSCIUTTO (2 TO 3 SLICES)

SERVES 4

Preheat oven to 425 degrees F.

Heat olive oil in a skillet over moderate heat. Add bread crumbs, stir to coat evenly with oil and cook, stirring often, until they are a deep golden brown, about 10 minutes. Season with salt and set aside.

Melt 2 tablespoons butter in a small saucepan over moderately low heat. Add flour and whisk to blend. Cook, stirring, 2 minutes, then add 1 cup milk, broth, bay leaf, thyme sprigs, garlic clove and salt and pepper to taste. Bring to a simmer, whisking. Adjust heat to maintain a gentle simmer and cook 15 minutes, whisking often. Scrape the sides and bottom of the pan occasionally with a spatula. Add a little more milk if béchamel gets too thick; it should be smooth and creamy, not thick or pasty.

Bring a pot of salted water to a boil over high heat. Add fennel bulbs and boil for 10 minutes, then drain. Pat bulbs dry, quarter them lengthwise and remove the cores. Slice lengthwise into thin strips.

Generously butter a shallow earthenware baking dish that measures approximately 12 by 7 inches. Arrange half the fennel in the baking dish in an even layer. Tear the prosciutto into shreds and arrange evenly over the fennel. Top with remaining fennel in an even layer. Using a fine-mesh sieve, strain the béchamel sauce evenly over the fennel. Top with browned bread crumbs. Bake 20 minutes. If desired, broil briefly to brown the top. Cool 10 minutes before serving.

spaghetti with sicilian green tomato sauce

When frost is imminent, growers will often pull the green tomatoes still on their vines and bring them to the farmers' market. San Francisco restaurateur Carlo Middione, an authority on southern Italian food, once told me that Sicilians make a pasta sauce with them, chopping them fine and mixing them with olive oil and garlic. I was intrigued enough by his description to try my own version. It is an exceptionally refreshing dish and one of the few pasta preparations that I enjoy at room temperature.

⅓ CUP PINE NUTS

1 POUND GREEN TOMATOES, PREFERABLY WITH SOME PINK BLUSH, VERY FINELY CHOPPED

½ CUP EXTRA VIRGIN OLIVE OIL

2 LARGE CLOVES GARLIC, MINCED

¼ TEASPOON HOT RED PEPPER FLAKES

1 POUND SPAGHETTI

SALT AND FRESHLY GROUND BLACK PEPPER

2 DOZEN FRESH BASIL LEAVES, TORN INTO SMALL PIECES

SERVES 4

Preheat oven to 325 degrees F. Toast pine nuts on a baking sheet until they are golden brown and fragrant, 12 to 15 minutes. Cool.

In a wide, shallow serving bowl, combine tomatoes, olive oil, garlic and hot-pepper flakes. You can make this mixture 1 to 2 hours ahead and let stand at room temperature. Do not add salt at this point as it will draw out the tomato juices.

Bring a large pot of salted water to a boil over high heat. Add pasta and cook until al dente. Just before spaghetti is ready, season sauce generously with salt and pepper and stir in basil leaves. Drain pasta and transfer to the serving bowl. Toss to coat with sauce. Scatter pine nuts on top.

autumn squash risotto with white truffle oil

Tiny bottles of aromatic white truffle oil have started to turn up in specialty stores at what seem like exorbitant prices. But it takes so little to flavor a dish that the price-per-serving is reasonable. Or so I tell myself. Drizzled lightly on a risotto with autumn squash and onions, the oil adds an earthy note that balances the vegetables' sweetness.

I like to use Butternut squash because it is easy to peel, but you could use any sweet hard-shelled squash you find at the farmers' market. Cooking the squash until it is tender before adding the rice ensures that it will be completely, meltingly soft when the risotto is finished. The squash should still be in recognizable pieces but ready to dissolve at the touch of a fork.

4 TABLESPOONS UNSALTED BUTTER
1 LARGE ONION, MINCED
½ POUND PEELED BUTTERNUT SQUASH, IN ⅓-INCH DICE
APPROXIMATELY 4½ CUPS LIGHT HOMEMADE CHICKEN BROTH, OR 2 CUPS LOW-SODIUM CANNED CHICKEN BROTH MIXED WITH 2½ CUPS WATER
1½ CUPS ARBORIO RICE
½ CUP DRY WHITE WINE
SALT AND FRESHLY GROUND BLACK PEPPER
¼ CUP FRESHLY GRATED PARMESAN CHEESE
1 TABLESPOON MINCED ITALIAN PARSLEY
WHITE TRUFFLE OIL

SERVES 4

Melt 3 tablespoons butter in a large pot over moderate heat. Add onion and saute until softened, about 10 minutes. Add squash and stir to coat with fat. Add ½ cup chicken broth, cover and adjust heat to maintain a simmer. Cook until squash is tender, about 10 minutes.

Put remaining broth in a small saucepan and bring to a simmer; adjust heat to keep broth hot but not boiling.

Add rice to onion and squash and cook, stirring, until rice is hot throughout. Add wine and cook, stirring, until wine is absorbed. Begin adding the hot broth ½ cup at a time, stirring frequently and waiting until each addition has been absorbed before adding more. Adjust heat so that mixture simmers gently, not vigorously. It should take 20 to 22 minutes for the rice to become al dente—firm to the tooth but with no hard core. The mixture should be creamy—neither soupy nor stiff. You may not need all the liquid; if you need a little more, use boiling water. Season with salt and pepper. Cover and let stand 3 minutes, then stir in remaining tablespoon butter, the cheese and the parsley.

Divide among 4 warm bowls. Top each serving with ½ teaspoon white truffle oil, but pass additional oil at the table for those who want more.

orecchiette with autumn squash, prosciutto, celery leaves and parmesan

At Da Tonino in Campobasso, capital of Italy's Molise region, the chef serves this sauce on homemade cavatelli. I loved the pungent taste of the celery leaves with the sweet autumn squash, and I have tried to duplicate the sauce as I remember it. At the farmers' market, look for Kabocha or Butternut squash, or ask for a squash with similarly sweet, dense flesh.

2 TABLESPOONS UNSALTED BUTTER

2 TABLESPOONS EXTRA VIRGIN OLIVE OIL

1 ONION, CHOPPED

2 OUNCES PROSCIUTTO DI PARMA, MINCED

1 POUND PEELED HARD-SHELLED SQUASH, IN ⅓-INCH DICE (SEE RECIPE INTRODUCTION)

½ POUND PLUM TOMATOES, PEELED, SEEDED AND FINELY CHOPPED

SALT AND FRESHLY GROUND BLACK PEPPER

½ CUP COARSELY CHOPPED PALE GREEN CELERY LEAVES, FROM THE INNER RIBS

1 POUND DRIED ORECCHIETTE, CONCHIGLIE OR CAVATELLI

⅔ CUP FRESHLY GRATED PARMESAN CHEESE

SERVES 4

Melt butter with oil in a 12-inch skillet over moderate heat. Add onion and saute until soft, about 10 minutes. Add prosciutto and saute 2 minutes. Add squash and tomatoes. Season with salt and pepper. Toss to coat with seasonings. Add ½ cup water. Cover and simmer gently until squash is tender, about 15 minutes. Stir in celery leaves.

Bring a large pot of salted water to a boil over high heat. Add pasta and cook until al dente. Drain pasta and return it to pot. Add sauce and cheese. Toss well, then serve on warm plates.

yellow split pea soup with autumn squash and kale

As most farmers' market shoppers discover, some of the best recipes are created spontaneously from items you find at the market together. In Northern California in autumn, that could mean tomatoes, squash, rosemary and kale—fine flavorings for a split pea soup.

Like all soups based on legumes, this one thickens considerably as it cools. If you make it ahead, you will need to thin it with a mixture of broth and water in equal amounts.

2 TABLESPOONS OLIVE OIL

2 TO 3 OUNCES PANCETTA, MINCED

1 LARGE ONION, MINCED

4 CLOVES GARLIC, MINCED

2 CUPS DRIED YELLOW SPLIT PEAS

1 FRESH ROSEMARY SPRIG, 4 INCHES LONG

4 CUPS HOMEMADE OR CANNED LOW-SODIUM CHICKEN BROTH, PLUS MORE IF NEEDED FOR THINNING

SALT AND FRESHLY GROUND BLACK PEPPER

½ POUND PEELED HARD-SHELLED SQUASH SUCH AS KABOCHA OR BUTTERNUT, IN ⅓-INCH DICE

½ POUND PLUM TOMATOES, PEELED, SEEDED AND DICED

⅓ POUND KALE OR GREEN CHARD, RIBS REMOVED

SERVES 6

Heat olive oil in a large pot over moderate heat. Add pancetta and saute until it renders some of its fat, about 3 minutes. Add onion and garlic and saute until onion is soft and sweet, about 10 minutes. Add split peas, rosemary, 4 cups chicken broth and 4 cups water. Bring to a simmer, cover and adjust heat to maintain a simmer. Cook until split peas are completely soft, 45 minutes to 1 hour. Taste often and remove rosemary sprig when rosemary flavor is strong enough. (It should be subtle.)

Season soup with salt and pepper. Stir in squash and tomatoes. Stack kale leaves a few at a time and slice into ribbons about ¼ inch wide. Stir them into the soup, cover and cook until squash and kale are tender, about 20 minutes. If soup is a little thick, thin with chicken broth. Taste and adjust seasoning before serving.

quick persimmon "ice cream"

When you find a good price at the farmers' market on Hachiya persimmons—the heart-shaped kind that must be soft before you eat them—buy some for the freezer. Let them ripen until completely soft at room temperature, then put them in the freezer, whole and unwrapped, where they will keep for weeks. When you crave a creamy dessert, take them out, cut them in chunks and puree them, fully frozen, in a food processor with buttermilk or half-and-half to make a velvety "ice cream." For a quick breakfast or lunch, use the same procedure but add enough buttermilk to make a smoothie.

2 RIPE HACHIYA PERSIMMONS
(ABOUT 1 POUND TOTAL), FROZEN
HARD
¼ CUP SUGAR
¼ TEASPOON VANILLA EXTRACT
½ CUP BUTTERMILK OR HALF-AND-
HALF
APPROXIMATELY 2 TEASPOONS
FRESH LEMON JUICE
GINGERSNAPS, OPTIONAL

SERVES 4

Quarter persimmons carefully with a heavy knife. Remove the stems and any seeds. Halve each quarter crosswise. Do not allow the persimmons to thaw even slightly.

Put the chunks in a food processor with the sugar and process until the persimmon is broken up into small pieces. With the motor running, add the vanilla and the buttermilk or half-and-half through the feed tube. Puree until smooth, stopping the machine to scrape down the sides once or twice. Add lemon juice to taste and puree again. Spoon into balloon wineglasses or compote dishes and serve immediately, with gingersnaps, if desired.

pomegranate apple jelly

This shimmering garnet jelly has an exquisite, exotic flavor. Spread it on toast or warm biscuits, or use it as a filling for baked apples. And take advantage of pomegranates' brief appearance at farmers' markets to make a few extra jars for holiday gifts. (Don't try to double this recipe, however; as with most jams and jellies, small batches work better.)

Cooking time will vary depending on the size of your pot. I use a wide pot to speed evaporation, so the juice jells more quickly and retains more of its fresh flavor. In any case, apples are high in pectin and their juice jells relatively fast. Test for doneness often so you catch the jelly at the proper moment, when it is quivering firm, not stiff.

2 POUNDS FRAGRANT APPLES SUCH AS GRAVENSTEINS

1 LARGE OR 2 MEDIUM POMEGRAN-ATES (TO YIELD ⅓ CUP JUICE)

2 TO 2¼ CUPS SUGAR

3 TO 4 TABLESPOONS STRAINED FRESH LEMON JUICE

MAKES 3 HALF-PINTS

Cut each apple into 8 wedges (do not core or peel). Combine apples and 4 cups water in a heavy saucepan and bring to a boil. Reduce heat and simmer until apples are very tender, stirring occasionally, about 40 minutes. Remove from heat, cover and let stand 8 hours.

Line a large sieve with a triple thickness of dampened cheesecloth; set over a large bowl. Pour apple mixture into sieve and press on the apple pieces with a wooden spoon to crush them and release more juice. Let drain overnight.

Without cutting the pomegranates, roll them firmly against a hard surface to break up the juice sacs inside. Take care not to pierce the skin anywhere or the juice—which stains—will spurt out. When the pomegranate is flaccid, indicating you have broken most of the juice sacs, pierce the skin with a knife and invert the pomegranate over a bowl; squeeze gently to release the juice. Strain the juice if necessary to remove any seeds or bits of pulp. You should have ⅓ cup.

Measure apple juice and transfer to a heavy, wide saucepan or skillet. Add ¾ cup sugar for each 1 cup juice. Mix in 3 tablespoons lemon juice. Cook over low heat, stirring, until sugar dissolves. Taste and add a little more lemon juice, if desired. Increase heat and bring to a boil. Adjust heat to maintain a simmer and cook, stirring occasionally, 10 minutes.

Add the pomegranate juice and simmer until mixture reaches the jelly stage, about 5 minutes. To test for doneness, remove pan from heat. Put a tablespoon of jelly on a chilled saucer and place in freezer for 2 minutes to chill quickly. Mixture should firm to a soft jelly consistency.

Skim off any foam on the surface of the jelly. Spoon hot jelly into clean, hot jars to within ½ inch from the top. Wipe rim clean with a towel dipped in hot water. Place lids and rings on jars and seal tightly. Cool and refrigerate for up to 3 months. Or, for longer storage, place just-filled jars in boiling water to cover by 1 inch and boil 15 minutes for half-pint jars, 20 minutes for pint jars. Transfer with tongs to a rack to cool; lids should form a seal. Sealed jars may be stored in a pantry for up to a year.

braised radicchio with raisins and pine nuts

Farmers' markets give growers a chance to try experimental crops on a small scale. They can get face-to-face feedback on flavor, and they don't have to be concerned about having enough to supply a distributor week after week. By now, even supermarkets carry the firm, round, pleasantly bitter heads of radicchio (*radicchio di Verona*), but you will probably have to shop a farmers' market to find the elongated *radicchio di Treviso*, a variety that the cognoscenti prize for its flavor.

This recipe is adapted from one in *Il radicchio rosso di Treviso* by Paolo Morganti. The combination of vinegar, sugar, raisins and pine nuts is common in Italy's Veneto region, where it is used with meats, fish and vegetables. Serve the braised radicchio as a first course, perhaps with some sliced prosciutto, or as a side dish with roast veal, duck or rabbit.

¼ CUP GOLDEN RAISINS

2 TABLESPOONS PINE NUTS

2 TABLESPOONS EXTRA VIRGIN OLIVE OIL

1 ONION, HALVED AND SLICED

3 TABLESPOONS WHITE WINE VINEGAR, PLUS MORE TO TASTE

1 TEASPOON SUGAR

1 POUND RADICCHIO, PREFERABLY TREVISO TYPE, QUARTERED LENGTHWISE

SALT AND FRESHLY GROUND BLACK PEPPER

1 TABLESPOON MINCED ITALIAN PARSLEY

SERVES 4

Put raisins in a small bowl, cover with warm water and let stand 30 minutes to soften. Preheat oven to 325 degrees F. Toast pine nuts on a baking sheet until golden brown and fragrant, 12 to 15 minutes.

Heat olive oil over moderate heat in a skillet large enough to hold all the radicchio in one layer. Add onion and saute until soft and sweet, about 10 minutes. Add 3 tablespoons vinegar and the sugar. Drain water from raisins and add additional water, if necessary, to make ¼ cup. Add water to skillet. Arrange radicchio in skillet cut side down. Season well with salt and pepper. Scatter the raisins over the radicchio. Cover, adjust heat to maintain a simmer and cook until radicchio is tender, about 15 minutes. Scatter the pine nuts over the radicchio, then remove from heat and let radicchio cool to room temperature in skillet.

To serve, spoon about half of the onions, raisins and pine nuts onto a serving platter. Arrange radicchio cut side up over the onions. Top with remaining onion, raisin and pine nut mixture. Taste and sprinkle with a little more vinegar if necessary. Garnish with parsley. Serve at room temperature.

fusilli "bella lecce"

This recipe is inspired by a dish I enjoyed at the Hotel President in Lecce, a richly baroque city in southern Italy. The sauce is something like a finely diced ratatouille, made with vegetables you are likely to find in the early autumn market. Chef Girardo Refolo served it on bucatini—hollow spaghettilike noodles—but it's also good on short pasta. Fusilli are particularly pleasing because the little bits of eggplant, tomato, bell pepper and zucchini slip down into the grooves.

3 TABLESPOONS EXTRA VIRGIN OLIVE OIL

½ ONION, MINCED

2 LARGE CLOVES GARLIC, MINCED

2 OUNCES PANCETTA, MINCED

1 POUND RIPE PLUM TOMATOES, PEELED AND DICED (NO NEED TO SEED)

¼ TEASPOON HOT RED PEPPER FLAKES, OR TO TASTE

¼ POUND JAPANESE OR ITALIAN EGGPLANT, UNPEELED, IN NEAT ¼-INCH DICE

½ RED BELL PEPPER, SEEDS AND RIBS REMOVED, IN NEAT ¼-INCH DICE

¼ POUND ZUCCHINI, IN NEAT ¼-INCH DICE

SALT TO TASTE

1 POUND DRIED FUSILLI

⅔ CUP FRESHLY GRATED PECORINO ROMANO CHEESE

SERVES 4 TO 6

Heat olive oil in a 12-inch skillet over moderately low heat. Add onion and garlic and saute until onion is soft, 8 to 10 minutes. Add pancetta and saute until it renders some of its fat, about 3 minutes, then add tomatoes and hot-pepper flakes. Raise heat to moderately high and cook, stirring often, until tomatoes collapse and begin to form a sauce, about 10 minutes. Add eggplant, bell pepper and zucchini. Season with salt. Saute 3 minutes. Add ½ cup water, cover, reduce heat to maintain a bare simmer and cook until vegetables are tender, about 10 minutes. Check occasionally and add more water if needed to achieve a saucelike consistency. Uncover, taste and adjust seasoning.

Bring a large pot of salted water to a boil over high heat. Add pasta and cook until al dente. Drain. Transfer to a warm bowl. Add sauce and cheese and toss well. Serve immediately on warm plates.

focaccette "ristorante ecco" with sweet peppers and olives

At Ristorante Ecco in San Francisco, chef and co-owner Susan Walter makes these immensely popular round *focaccette* (small focaccia) for patrons of her restaurant's lunchtime takeaway window. In summer she tops them with halved plum tomatoes slow-cooked until they are intense and sweet. Sometimes she tops the dough with golden raisins, sugar and pine nuts. I have adapted Susan's recipe for a home kitchen. She, in turn, says her inspiration was a recipe in Carol Field's book, *Focaccia*. In season, you could replace the peppers with zucchini, eggplant, mushrooms, leeks, or whatever strikes your fancy at the farmers' market.

This dough is so moist that it is best to make it in an electric mixer with a paddle. Resist the temptation to add more flour. The wet dough is responsible for the pleasing texture of the finished bread. These *focaccette* are ideal for picnics or potlucks because they can be baked a few hours ahead and transported easily.

FOR THE SPONGE:

1 CUP WARM WATER
ONE ¼-OUNCE PACKAGE OR
2½ TEASPOONS ACTIVE DRY YEAST
1 CUP UNBLEACHED ALL-PURPOSE
FLOUR

FOR THE DOUGH:

SPONGE (SEE ABOVE)
⅓ CUP DRY WHITE WINE
⅓ CUP OLIVE OIL
1 TABLESPOON KOSHER SALT
2 TABLESPOONS CORNMEAL
2¾ CUPS UNBLEACHED
ALL-PURPOSE FLOUR, PLUS MORE
FOR SHAPING

FOR THE SEASONED OIL:

½ CUP EXTRA VIRGIN OLIVE OIL
1 LARGE CLOVE GARLIC, MINCED
¼ TEASPOON HOT RED
PEPPER FLAKES
¾ TEASPOON KOSHER SALT
1½ TABLESPOONS CHOPPED
ITALIAN PARSLEY

FOR THE TOPPING:

1 LARGE RED BELL PEPPER
1 LARGE GREEN BELL PEPPER
1 LARGE GOLD BELL PEPPER
2 TABLESPOONS PLUS 2 TEASPOONS
OLIVE OIL
SALT
1 SMALL ONION, HALVED AND
SLICED

To make the sponge: One day ahead, put the warm water in a medium bowl. Sprinkle yeast over surface and let stand 2 minutes, then whisk with a fork until dissolved. Add flour and stir with a wooden spoon until smooth. Cover and let stand at room temperature for 24 hours.

To make the dough: Put sponge in a heavy-duty mixer with a paddle attachment. Add ½ cup water, wine, olive oil, salt and cornmeal. With the mixer running, gradually add the 2¾ cups flour to make a soft dough. The dough will hold together but will be moist and a little sticky. Knead in mixer for 5 minutes with paddle attachment. Scrape down the sides and the paddle, cover the bowl with plastic wrap and let dough rise 1½ hours.

Turn out the dough onto a floured work surface; the dough will be sticky. Divide it into 10 equal pieces, sprinkling them lightly with flour to keep them from sticking to the board or your hands.

15 BLACK OLIVES SUCH AS KALAMATA OR GAETA, PITTED AND HALVED

¼ CUP FRESHLY GRATED PARMESAN CHEESE

MAKES 10 FOCACCETTE

Gently shape the pieces into flattened rounds. They don't need to be precise; a somewhat rough, handmade look is part of their charm. Place the rounds on two lightly oiled heavy baking sheets, cover with a towel and let rise 1½ hours.

To make the seasoned oil: In a small bowl, combine all ingredients. Let stand at least 30 minutes to marry the flavors.

To make the topping: Cut a thin slice off the stem end of each bell pepper. With a small knife, cut away and remove the core. Shake out any loose seeds and trim away as much of the white ribs as you can. Slice the cored peppers crosswise into rings about ¼ inch wide. You will need 10 rings from each pepper; save any remaining rings for a salad.

Heat 2 tablespoons olive oil in a large skillet over moderate heat. Add pepper rings, season with salt and saute until slightly softened, 5 to 8 minutes. Remove them with tongs to a plate as they soften. You don't want them to color or wilt. Add remaining 2 teaspoons oil to pan. When hot, add onion and saute until soft, 5 to 10 minutes. Transfer to another plate.

Position a rack in the center of the oven. Line oven rack with baking tiles or a baking stone. Preheat oven to 550 degrees F or highest setting for at least 45 minutes.

Dimple dough rounds vigorously with lightly floured fingertips, then apply toppings: put a few of the onion slices on each round, then one each of the red, green and gold pepper rings. The pepper rings should overlap slightly, like the Olympic Games symbol. Put 3 olive halves on each round. Brush with seasoned oil, making sure to get some of the seasonings on each round. (Reserve some of the oil for brushing on the rounds after baking.) Divide the cheese among the 10 rounds, sprinkling it evenly over each.

Bake 1 sheet at a time until golden brown, about 8 minutes. Transfer to a rack. Brush the edges of the *focaccette* with the remaining seasoned oil. Cool slightly before serving.

bruschetta with sweet peppers and ricotta

Each year at the farmers' market seems to bring bell peppers in ever more stunning colors. By mid-September, Bay Area markets are ablaze with red, yellow, green and orange peppers and multicolored combinations thereof. I can't resist them. To show off their colors, I'll braise them together, then spoon them over ricotta-topped *bruschetta* (oiled toast).

You may need to explore the breads available in your area to find the ideal one for *bruschetta* (pronounced brew-sketta). If the bread is too dense, the *bruschetta* will be hard to eat; if the bread is too holey, it won't support the topping. Look for a rustic country-style loaf made of nothing but flour, water, yeast and salt. Once toasted, it should be sturdy enough to stand up to a slathering of ricotta and juicy peppers. Offer these Italian toasts at the start of a meal with a glass of crisp white wine.

1 LARGE RED BELL PEPPER
1 LARGE GOLDEN BELL PEPPER
¼ CUP EXTRA VIRGIN OLIVE OIL
1 LARGE CLOVE GARLIC, MINCED
SALT AND FRESHLY GROUND
BLACK PEPPER
6 SLICES COUNTRY-STYLE BREAD,
EACH ABOUT ½ INCH THICK AND 4
INCHES LONG
¼ POUND WHOLE-MILK RICOTTA
CHEESE
6 TO 8 FRESH BASIL LEAVES, TORN
INTO SMALL PIECES

158

SERVES 6

Roast peppers over a gas flame or charcoal fire, or under a broiler, until blackened on all sides. Transfer to a plastic bag and close the bag so peppers steam as they cool. When cool enough to handle, peel the peppers, halve them and remove seeds and ribs. Cut peppers lengthwise into strips ½ to ¾ inch wide.

Heat 2 tablespoons olive oil in a skillet over moderate heat. Add garlic and saute until lightly colored, about 2 minutes. Add peppers, season with salt and pepper and saute just until peppers are coated with oil and are hot throughout. Remove from heat and cool in pan. For best flavor, saute peppers 1 hour ahead so they can absorb the oil and exude their own juices.

Toast the bread on both sides in a broiler, toaster oven, on a stove-top grill or—the best choice—over a charcoal fire. Remove from heat and drizzle one side of each slice with 1 teaspoon oil. Season ricotta with salt and pepper, then spread an even layer of cheese on each of the 6 toasts. Stir the basil into the peppers, then divide the peppers and their juices among the 6 toasts. Serve hot.

sweet potato and chestnut soup

Why amplify the sweet potato's natural sweetness by adding sugar, as so many recipes do? I'd rather emphasize the vegetable's subtle nuttiness—in this case, by pairing it with chestnuts in a smooth, earthy soup. Ask at the farmers' market for a dry-fleshed sweet potato, the kind that usually has yellow (not orange) flesh.

Serve this soup for a simple dinner with an endive and apple salad first and some cheese for dessert. Or offer small portions as a first course in a more elaborate holiday meal.

¾ POUND FRESH CHESTNUTS OR 18 ROASTED, PEELED AND DRY-PACKED WHOLE BOTTLED CHESTNUTS (ABOUT 6 OUNCES)

3 TABLESPOONS UNSALTED BUTTER

1 LARGE ONION, MINCED

1 POUND DRY-FLESHED SWEET POTA-TOES (SEE RECIPE INTRODUCTION), PEELED, IN ½-INCH DICE

1 TEASPOON MINCED FRESH THYME

SALT AND FRESHLY GROUND BLACK PEPPER

APPROXIMATELY 2½ CUPS HOME-MADE OR CANNED LOW-SODIUM CHICKEN BROTH

½ CUP HEAVY CREAM

2 TABLESPOONS CRÈME FRAÎCHE, OPTIONAL

2 TABLESPOONS THINLY SLICED FRESH CHIVES, OPTIONAL

SERVES 4

If using fresh chestnuts: Cut an X in the flat side of each chestnut, then boil the chestnuts for 10 minutes. With a slotted spoon, lift them out of hot water one at a time. (They are easier to peel when hot.) Cradle them in a dish towel to protect your hands, then squeeze them gently and peel back from the X, removing the hard shell and the papery brown skin. The nuts may crumble, but that's okay. Coarsely chop any large pieces.

If using bottled chestnuts, inspect them and remove any skin still clinging to them. Chop coarsely.

Melt butter in a large pot over moderately low heat. Add onion and saute until soft and sweet, about 10 minutes. Add sweet potatoes, chestnuts and thyme. Season with salt and pepper. Cook, stirring occasionally, for about 5 minutes, then add 2 cups chicken broth and 2 cups water. Cover, adjust heat to maintain a simmer and cook until chestnuts and sweet potatoes are tender, about 15 minutes.

Pass mixture through a food mill into a bowl, or puree in a food processor. Return to a clean pot and stir in cream. Reheat, thinning as needed with a mixture of broth and water in equal amounts. Taste and adjust seasoning.

Divide among 4 warm bowls. Top each serving with a drizzle of crème fraîche and a sprinkling of chives, if desired.

provençal vegetable soup

Seeing fresh cranberry beans at the farmers' market makes me hungry for vegetable soup. Inside their cranberry-and-cream pods are beautiful purple-streaked beans that Italians prize for minestrone and Provençal cooks use in their famous *soupe au pistou*. *Pistou* is the French version of pesto, an aromatic basil sauce that, when stirred in at the last minute, lifts a simple vegetable soup out of the ordinary.

1 POUND FRESH UNSHELLED CRAN-
BERRY BEANS OR OTHER SHELLING
BEANS

½ ONION

FOR THE PISTOU:

1 CUP TIGHTLY BACKED FRESH BASIL
LEAVES

1 LARGE CLOVE GARLIC, THINLY
SLICED

⅓ CUP EXTRA VIRGIN OLIVE OIL

¼ CUP FRESHLY GRATED PARMESAN
CHEESE

SALT AND FRESHLY GROUND
BLACK PEPPER

2 TABLESPOONS EXTRA VIRGIN
OLIVE OIL

2 TO 3 OUNCES PANCETTA, DICED

1 LARGE ONION, MINCED

1 POUND PLUM TOMATOES, PEELED,
SEEDED AND DICED

3 CUPS HOMEMADE OR CANNED
LOW-SODIUM CHICKEN BROTH, PLUS
MORE IF NEEDED

½ POUND GREEN BEANS, ENDS
TRIMMED, IN ½-INCH LENGTHS

½ POUND BAKING POTATOES,
PEELED, IN ½-INCH DICE

2 ZUCCHINI, QUARTERED LENGTH-
WISE, THEN CUT CROSSWISE IN
½-INCH-WIDE PIECES

¼ POUND DRIED ELBOW MACARONI
OR OTHER SMALL PASTA

SERVES 6

Shell the beans; you should have about 1½ cups. Combine beans and onion in a saucepan with salted water to cover. Bring to a simmer over high heat, then adjust heat to maintain a simmer. Cook until beans are barely tender, 20 to 25 minutes. Remove from heat and cool in liquid. (They will continue to cook as they cool, and they will cook some more in the soup.)

Meanwhile, make *pistou:* Put basil and garlic in food processor and process until well chopped, scraping down sides of bowl once or twice. With motor running, add oil through the feed tube; blend well, scraping down sides of bowl once or twice. Add cheese and blend again. Transfer to a bowl and stir in salt and pepper to taste. If made ahead, cover with plastic wrap, pressing directly onto surface to prevent browning.

Heat olive oil in a large soup pot over moderate heat. Add pancetta and saute until it renders some of its fat, about 3 minutes. Add onion and saute until soft, about 10 minutes. Add tomatoes and saute, stirring often, until they soften, about 10 minutes. Add 3 cups broth and 3 cups water. Bring mixture to a simmer. Add green beans, cover partially, adjust heat to maintain a gentle simmer and cook 15 minutes. Add potatoes and simmer 15 minutes. Add zucchini and simmer 10 minutes.

Drain cranberry beans and add them to soup pot along with pasta. Cook, uncovered, until pasta is just tender, 10 to 12 minutes. Thin soup, if desired, with a little chicken broth, but it should be thick with vegetables. Season with salt and pepper. Cover and let stand 5 minutes before serving in warm bowls. Top each serving with about 1 teaspoon of *pistou* and pass the rest.

pear sorbet with pear eau-de-vie

Pears have a narrow window of perfect ripeness. If you overbuy, consider making a sorbet to preserve the fruit's flavor. Thanks to the alcohol in this recipe, the sorbet stays soft for days. I originally attempted to make it with uncooked pear, to retain the most flavor, but the pureed fresh fruit turned brown. Through Lindsey Shere's book, *Chez Panisse Desserts*, I learned that you have to cook the pear a little to keep the sorbet pale. The brief cooking does not diminish the flavor. Serve in wineglasses or glass compote dishes.

3 POUNDS RIPE PEARS, PREFERABLY COMICE

APPROXIMATELY 1½ CUPS SUGAR

¼ CUP STRAINED FRESH LEMON JUICE

2 TABLESPOONS PEAR EAU-DE-VIE, PLUS MORE AT SERVING TIME

MAKES ABOUT 5 CUPS, TO SERVE 10

Quarter, core and peel the pears. Cut them in large chunks and place in a saucepan with ¼ cup water. Cover and bring to a simmer over moderate heat. Simmer gently until pears are cooked through, about 10 minutes. Transfer pears and any liquid in pan to a food processor and process until smooth. Measure the volume of pear puree. You should have about 4 cups.

Return the puree to the food processor and add sugar in the proportion of 1½ cups sugar to 4 cups puree. Add lemon juice and pear eau-de-vie and process until mixture is completely smooth and sugar has dissolved. Transfer to a bowl and refrigerate until well chilled.

Freeze in an ice cream maker according to manufacturer's directions. Because of alcohol, sorbet will not freeze hard.

To serve, put ½ cup sorbet in each serving bowl or glass. Spoon 1½ teaspoons additional pear eau-de-vie over each portion.

autumn fruit with ricotta, honey and poppy seeds

Paul Ferrari, owner of Ultra Lucca Delicatessens in the San Francisco Bay Area, gave me the idea of topping fresh ricotta with honey and poppy seeds—a presentation he encountered in Tuscany. Paul sells a honey with bits of chestnut mixed in, which would be exquisite here, but any good honey will do. Serve the drizzled ricotta with sliced autumn fruits from the farmers' market, such as apples, pears, figs or Fuyu persimmons.

4 LARGE FRESH GRAPE LEAVES, OPTIONAL

1 ⅓ CUPS WHOLE-MILK RICOTTA CHEESE

APPROXIMATELY 2 TABLESPOONS HONEY, OR MORE TO TASTE

POPPY SEEDS

SUGGESTED AUTUMN FRUITS:

1 APPLE OR PEAR, QUARTERED, CORED AND SLICED

1 FUYU PERSIMMON, PEELED AND SLICED

4 LARGE FRESH FIGS, QUARTERED

If using, place a grape leaf on each of 4 plates. Top each grape leaf with ⅓ cup ricotta. Drizzle the ricotta with ½ tablespoon honey, or more, if desired. Sprinkle generously with poppy seeds.

On the other side of the plate, arrange sliced fruits: apple or pear, persimmon and/or quartered figs. Alternatively, serve both the cheese and the fruit family style on platters.

163

SERVES 4

THE MARKET IN

winter

In mild climates, the winter market provides plenty of inspiration for a diner hungry for more substantial fare. Root vegetables dominate many growers' displays, volunteering their earthy sweetness for soups, purees and stews. The knobby celery root makes an appearance, enticing those who love its clean celery flavor to plan a celery and apple salad or steamed mussels with diced celery root. Parsnip fans—and there are many—look forward to roasting the sweet roots tucked around a chicken or whipping them into a smooth puree with potatoes. Rutabagas lure takers who appreciate the character they add to a turkey vegetable soup or a root vegetable hash.

Nature has seen to it that at least some green vegetables can withstand cold—if not freezing—weather. Winter market shoppers will probably find hefty green cabbages to shred for soups and crunchy slaws or to steam in wedges, and the delicate Savoy cabbage which, braised until soft, enhances risotto. Beloved by Italians but new to most Americans, broccoli rabe also enlivens winter, offering the possibility of pairing it with orecchiette (ear-shaped pasta) or with panfried sausage or steamed clams. Mounds of white-shanked leeks make their way into shoppers' bags, destined for soup, for leeks vinaigrette or for a baked gratin with cream.

The market knows no shortage of sturdy leafy greens in winter, including those—like collards and kale—that frost sweetens. Braised with chick-peas, wilted in a hot bacon dressing or stirred into a white bean soup, these greens add nutrition, flavor and variety to the table.

For fruit, the shopper turns to the enticing array of citrus—navel oranges, blood oranges, Valencia oranges, mandarin oranges, grapefruits and the puffy, thick-skinned pomelos. For launching a wholesome breakfast or ending a dinner on a refreshing note, these winter fruits have few equals.

broccoli rabe

Perhaps because of the growth of Italian restaurants in this country, broccoli rabe is surging in popularity, too. Italians love it, sauteing it in olive oil with garlic and hot-pepper flakes, then tossing it with pasta or serving it with panfried sausage. Although it looks like a broccoli relative, with deep blue-green leaves, thin stems and small florets, it is botanically closer to a turnip, appreciated for its leaves and stems, not its root. You may also see it called rape, rapini or raab in books and in markets.

By any name, broccoli rabe has a pronounced bitter taste that may take getting used to. Cook it with other strong flavors, such as anchovies, garlic, olives and pecorino cheese, then juxtapose it with something soothing like polenta or pasta.

selection: Broccoli rabe should look perky and have deep green color, tender stems and few or no yellow flowers.

storage: Store it in a loose plastic bag in the refrigerator crisper and use quickly.

cabbage

Whether shredded and eaten raw as a crunchy salad, steamed in butter with paprika, or stuffed and braised, fresh cabbage adds welcome variety to winter meals. Easy to grow and undemanding, it gives a farmer some breathing room because it doesn't demand to be picked the moment it's mature. Some varieties store well on the plant, becoming, if anything, even sweeter in cold weather.

For culinary purposes, it helps to divide cabbages into three distinct groups: green heading, red heading and Savoy. (I am leaving aside the several types of Chinese cabbage, which I don't know well.) The familiar heavy green headers are perfect for homemade sauerkraut, coleslaw and dishes requiring long, slow braising. Red heading cabbages lend themselves to braising with bacon and red wine, with grated fresh apples or pears, or with dried fruit. Because red cabbages have thicker, sturdier leaves, they take longer to cook than the other types. In contrast, Savoy cabbage cooks quickly because its crinkly pale green leaves are thin and more loosely layered. These delicate leaves foretell the mild, sweet flavor that makes this cabbage a European favorite.

Just-picked cabbage may not be subject to rapid decline like corn and peas, but it does lose moisture in a cooler. At Coke Farm in San Juan Bautista, California, workers harvest cabbage for the farmers' market at least once or twice a week so that it doesn't sit in a cooler too long. That way, says owner Christine Coke, farmers' market shoppers are likely to get a sweeter, crisper, juicier cabbage than they would find at a grocery store.

selection: Cabbage should have good, bright color and feel firm and heavy for its size. A just-picked red cabbage, in particular, will have an intense color, says Coke. A moist-looking butt might also indicate a fresh-cut cabbage; then again, it's possible to keep trimming the butt so that it just looks fresh.

storage: Store cabbage in a plastic bag in the refrigerator crisper.

celery root

With its mellow celery flavor and crisp, applelike texture, celery root (also called celeriac) is high on my list of vegetables that American cooks should know better. It is well regarded in France, where many home kitchens have a special grater for making the matchstick-sized pieces needed for *céleri rémoulade*—raw celery root marinated in a thick, mustardy mayonnaise. French home cooks puree celery root with potatoes, or layer it with sliced potatoes in a gratin, or make a potato-thickened, cream-enriched celery root soup.

When freshly harvested, celery root is at its most appealing. It gradually loses moisture, and therefore texture, says California grower Kachi Takahashi. Bought at the farmers' market, celery root is likely to be firm, moist and crisp. Bought at the grocery store, the much-older celery root may be spongy. "It's like a crisp, new apple versus a storage apple," says Takahashi. At the farmers' market, the celerylike tops are usually attached to prove that the root was recently harvested.

selection: Roots should feel firm and have fresh-looking tops, if attached. Celery root is often rather hairy and gnarly; that's not a sign of poor quality but it does mean you will have to trim a lot. If possible, choose roots that are more uniform so you will have a higher yield. The root's size says little about its quality, although large ones sometimes have a hollow or pithy center.

storage: Takahashi recommends wrapping celery root in a damp paper towel before refrigerating it in the vegetable crisper.

citrus

In mid-winter, when even California farmers' markets become a shadow of their summer selves, citrus fruits save the day. As juice, as a breakfast fruit, or as part of a dessert or salad, they refresh our palates and provide relief from rich winter food. The Chinese eat tangerines and pomelos at New Year's to bring good fortune, and even to me, citrus fruits convey a sense of prosperity. When I go to the trouble to make fresh-squeezed tangerine or blood orange juice in the morning, I feel like I am having a breakfast fit for a queen.

Farmers' market oranges and grapefruits may not look any different from the fruit at the grocery store, but chances are they are a great deal fresher. "The citrus you buy at the farmers' market, at least from me, is picked one day and on your table within a day or two," says Bob Polito, a California grower. Citrus intended for supermarkets typically goes from the field to a packing house, where it can sit for a while; then into a cooler, where it can sit for a while; then to the grocery store via truck. "In storage, it just gets old," says Polito. "So often, when people look at my grapefruit, they say, 'Gee, these are really hard.' They're used to soft, spongy fruit from the grocery store."

The longer citrus hangs on the tree, the sweeter it gets; early-season fruit is rarely first-rate. "A lot of times, the stuff you get in the store is picked too early," says Polito. Growers trying to rush the first navel oranges to market to get the best price will pick them as soon as the oranges meet the industry sugar standard.

Everyone is familiar with seedless navel oranges and thin-skinned Valencia juice oranges. For eating out of hand or adding to a child's lunchbox, look for the easy-peeling seedless Satsuma mandarins. Mandarins—some varieties of which are called tangerines—make marvelous juice. So do blood oranges, and rising production means they are no longer an extravagance. Among grapefruits, try the Oroblanco, a low-acid, white-fleshed cross between a grapefruit and a pomelo. Meyer lemons, a popular backyard fruit in California, are now being cultivated by several growers and turning up at farmers' markets; the Meyer's low-acid juice and fragrant peel make exquisite ice cream, custard, lemon curd and lemon meringue pie.

selection: Look for citrus fruits that feel heavy for their size. Heaviness indicates high juice content. Grapefruits—the Oroblanco excepted—should have thin skins. Even Bob

Polito admits it's not always easy to recognize good citrus by eye, aroma or touch. Fortunately, at the farmers' market, you can almost always get a taste.

storage: Store citrus fruits in a cool place or in the refrigerator. Don't leave them in plastic bags.

greens for cooking

Long after the fair-weather farmers' market fans have gone home for the season, those of us who love leafy greens still turn up with our canvas bags. The tomatoes and corn are just a memory when the market fills with cold-weather alternatives: kale, collards, chard, dandelion, mustard and turnip greens, all of them capable of withstanding a chill. In fact, many people say that frost sweetens greens, especially kale and collards. "My European customers won't buy kale until there's been a frost," says California grower Sue Temple.

Although these greens differ in appearance, flavor, texture and cooking time, they share enough characteristics to discuss them together. All of them prefer cool weather, becoming tough or bolting when the weather turns hot. (Chard is the exception; it can take some heat, although not a lot.) All of them, when mature, require some cooking, although young dandelion greens are enjoyable raw in salads.

You will probably find a much larger array of these nutritious greens at a farmers' market than you will at a grocery store. Grocery stores are reluctant to give space to vegetables that don't move quickly, and goodness knows, Americans are not clamoring for dandelion greens. But diversified growers who work the farmers' markets are happy to sell only 10 or 20 bunches a day to aficionados who appreciate the greens' fine flavor.

A few descriptive comments may help you identify them at the market:

KALE The most familiar form has sturdy, crinkly blue-green leaves and tough round ribs. Red Russian kale has a flatter blue-green leaf that turns purplish red and quite sweet in cold weather.

COLLARDS Thick, flat, leathery, almost fanlike blue-green leaves are attached to hard round stems. Their flavor is strong and earthy.

CHARD Perhaps the chard most familiar to shoppers has thick, wide cream-colored ribs and elongated, veined dark green leaves. Other varieties have red ribs and red-veined green leaves or even beet-red leaves. Chard's flavor is perhaps the mildest of all the cooking greens. It is never peppery or pungent, but more typically gentle, even sweet.

DANDELION GREENS Long, green and skinny with a sawtooth edge, the leaves can be peppery, the more so the larger they get.

MUSTARD GREENS The thin, elongated, yellow-green leaves have frilly edges and a peppery bite that gets sharper with age.

TURNIP GREENS Usually darker and more lobed than mustard greens, turnip greens have a similar elongated shape. They are mild when young, more aggressive with age.

If boiled in water or a flavorful broth, the more delicate greens—chard, dandelion greens and mustard greens—take only about 5 minutes to cook. For sturdier greens such as kale, collards and turnip greens, figure anywhere from 20 to 40 minutes.

selection: It sounds self-evident that greens should look fresh, but that's essential. Once harvested, they begin to lose their natural moisture. So look for greens that are turgid, with no sign of yellowing. Chard leaves should be shiny, but other greens won't be. In general, for all greens, small leaves will be more delicate in flavor and texture than large ones. With chard, I always look for ribs that look tender, too, because I like to use them.

storage: Greens need to be prevented from drying out, says Temple. Keep them in a closed plastic bag in the refrigerator crisper. They will stay fresh longer if you use a sturdy store-bought plastic bag with a closure, not the thin giveaway kind.

leeks

Belying their delicate onion flavor, leeks are rugged vegetables capable of overwintering in icy ground. Ellen and Shepherd Ogden, who operate The Cook's Garden nursery in Vermont, say they have sometimes had to melt the frozen soil around their leeks before they could harvest them. But in the kitchen, they seem more fragile, quickly softening when braised and contributing a sweet background flavor to dishes.

The white and pale green shank of the leek is the edible part; the green leaves are tough and good only for the stockpot or compost pile. Some varieties—King Richard is one—

produce extra-long shanks that yield a high proportion of edible part. You may pay more for them, but they are probably a better buy.

Because of the way leeks grow, dirt often gets trapped between the leaves, and a little grit can ruin a dish. To wash them, swish the sliced leeks in a large bowl or sink full of water, then lift them out, leaving the dirt behind. If cooking leeks whole, slit them lengthwise, cutting several inches into the pale green part of the shank, then open under running water and let the water wash between the leaves.

Leeks are harvested year-round in some climates. They are typically planted in spring and fall and, depending on the variety, harvested 75 to 145 days later. In summer, however, too much warm weather will cause them to push up a seed stalk, which ruins them for most uses.

selection: Leeks should have fresh-looking tops and several inches of white shank. Slender ones are usually more tender. Especially in summer, watch out for leeks that have formed a tough central seed stalk. It's hard to tell by eye, but sometimes you can feel the hardness within the leek. If you plan to cook the leeks whole, try to buy ones of comparable thickness so they cook evenly.

storage: Keep leeks in an open plastic bag in the refrigerator crisper.

parsnips

You can't hurry a parsnip. This sweet, cream-colored root vegetable is slow to germinate and slow to grow; seeded in spring, it may need six months to reach harvestable size. Even then, it would happily stay in the ground longer, becoming sweeter if hit by frost. Some say the tastiest parsnips are those that overwinter in the frozen ground and are pulled before they start to grow again in the spring.

But most parsnip fans work up an appetite for the vegetable in late fall and winter. In many homes, parsnips are a holiday tradition, roasted alongside the prime rib, glazed like carrots or whipped with butter and cream. When cooked, their creamy texture and sweet, nutty flavor resemble those of a dry-fleshed sweet potato. The central core is sometimes woody and must be trimmed away, but if the root is of a decent size, plenty of edible flesh remains.

selection: Choose parsnips that feel somewhat rigid; if they are at all flabby, they have probably been out of the ground awhile and lost moisture. Parsnips also tend to yellow a little in storage, says California grower Paul Holmes; whiter parsnips are likely to be fresher. Compared to carrots, which they resemble, parsnips have broader shoulders and skinnier tips; I try to choose those that have the most gradual tapering so that I can get more uniform pieces. Although jumbo parsnips can be sweet, they tend to have a high proportion of woody core.

storage: Keep parsnips in an open plastic bag in the refrigerator crisper.

rutabagas

A popular bumper sticker in California, usually spotted on the back of a decrepit Volkswagen bus, says, "Give peas a chance." I'd like to make the same plea for rutabagas; if people would try them with an open mind, they would surely like them. California grower Frances Andrews tells me that she and her husband gave rutabagas away at the farmers' market the first year they grew them. But customers reported back that they liked them, and the next year, people asked for them.

These thick-skinned golden roots with the purple shoulders have an image problem, not a flavor problem. If carefully grown and properly cooked, they are carrot-sweet and slightly peppery, with a golden flesh that tastes like a cross between a turnip and a yellow-fleshed sweet potato. Thickly peeled, then cubed and boiled, rutabagas can be mashed with butter, salt and pepper. They can also be mixed with other root vegetables—potatoes, parsnips, carrots—to make vegetable hash, or coated with olive oil and roasted alongside these same kin. In supermarkets, produce managers discard the greens because they deteriorate much faster than the roots, but Andrews tells me that the greens are tasty. She brings them, bunched, to the farmers' market.

Rutabagas store well in the ground, even tolerating a frost, so growers don't have to harvest them all at once. They also do well in carefully controlled cold storage, lasting into spring.

selection: A rutabaga should feel firm and have a smooth skin that shows no sign of wrinkling, an indication of moisture loss. Big versus small? There's no consensus. "I think they develop more flavor when they get bigger," says Andrews. "When they're little, they don't taste like much of anything. A large grapefruit size is perfect." In my experience, larger rutabagas tend to be more peppery and sometimes woody; I go for the smaller ones.

storage: The ideal place for rutabagas is a cool, dark, humid root cellar. Lacking that, refrigerate them in a plastic bag to keep moisture in.

clams with broccoli rabe and sausage

Little known by non-Italians a decade ago, broccoli rabe is winning fans at the farmers' market. More and more shoppers appreciate its pleasantly bitter taste and its compatibility with southern Italian ingredients. A Neapolitan chef in San Francisco told me he grew up on broccoli rabe with garlic and panfried sausage. In this recipe, broccoli rabe, garlic and spicy sausage create a lusty topping for small clams steamed in white wine. In place of dried sausage, you could use fresh hot Italian fennel sausage removed from its casing and crumbled with a fork. Be sure to have crusty bread on the table for soaking up the flavorful clam broth.

1 TO 1¼ POUNDS BROCCOLI RABE
2 TABLESPOONS OLIVE OIL
1 ONION, CHOPPED
4 CLOVES GARLIC, MINCED
¼ POUND DRIED PORK SAUSAGE
SUCH AS LINGUIÇA OR SPANISH-
STYLE CHORIZO
1 CUP DRY WHITE WINE
2 POUNDS SMALL CLAMS, SCRUBBED
CLEAN, TIGHTLY CLOSED

SERVES 4

Trim the broccoli rabe by removing or paring any stems bigger than a pencil and discarding any thin stems that feel tough. Cut remaining florets and stems into 2- to 3-inch pieces. You should have about ¾ pound.

Heat the olive oil in a large pot over moderately low heat. Add the onion and garlic and saute until onion is soft and sweet, about 10 minutes. Quarter the sausage lengthwise, then cut crosswise into ¼-inch pieces. Add to skillet and saute for a couple of minutes to release some of its fat. Add white wine and raise heat to moderately high. Simmer for 30 to 45 seconds to burn off the alcohol, then add the clams. Scatter broccoli rabe on top and cover. Cook, shaking pot once or twice to redistribute the clams, until the clams open and the broccoli rabe is tender, about 5 minutes. Divide among 4 warm bowls, discarding any clams that did not open.

potato soup with savoy cabbage and prosciutto

Made with a sweet Savoy cabbage from the farmers' market, a potato and cabbage soup banishes any notion of winter as a time of privation.

4 TABLESPOONS UNSALTED BUTTER

1 LARGE ONION, CHOPPED

2 LARGE CLOVES GARLIC, MINCED

2 OUNCES PROSCIUTTO DI PARMA, CHOPPED

1 TABLESPOON MINCED FRESH SAGE

1 TEASPOON MINCED FRESH ROSE-MARY

2 POUNDS BAKING POTATOES, PEELED, IN ½-INCH CUBES

SALT AND FRESHLY GROUND BLACK PEPPER

2 CUPS HOMEMADE OR CANNED LOW-SODIUM CHICKEN BROTH

¾ POUND SAVOY CABBAGE, FINELY SLICED

SERVES 6

Melt butter in a large pot over moderate heat. Add onion, garlic, prosciutto, sage and rosemary. Saute until onion is soft and sweet, about 10 minutes. Add potatoes, season with salt and pepper and stir to coat with seasonings. Saute about 3 minutes, then add broth and 4 cups water. Bring to a simmer, cover and adjust heat to maintain a gentle simmer. Cook until potatoes are tender, about 20 minutes.

Using a potato masher, mash potatoes until most of them break down and begin to thicken the soup; it's nice to leave a few slightly rough pieces to give the soup a more interesting texture. Stir in cabbage and simmer gently until it is just tender, about 10 minutes. Taste and adjust seasoning.

risotto with savoy cabbage, lemon and parsley

A ruffled Savoy cabbage has the sweet flavor and delicate texture required here; the common smooth heading cabbage would be too strong. Braised with onion first, then cooked with the rice, the delicate Savoy almost melts into the risotto, leaving its sweetness behind.

2 TABLESPOONS UNSALTED BUTTER

3 TABLESPOONS EXTRA VIRGIN OLIVE OIL

1 ONION, CHOPPED

¾ POUND SAVOY CABBAGE, CORED AND THINLY SLICED

SALT AND FRESHLY GROUND BLACK PEPPER

4½ CUPS LIGHT HOMEMADE CHICKEN BROTH, OR 2 CUPS CANNED LOW-SODIUM CHICKEN BROTH MIXED WITH 2½ CUPS WATER

1½ CUPS ARBORIO RICE

½ CUP DRY WHITE WINE

¼ TEASPOON GRATED LEMON ZEST, OR MORE TO TASTE

2 TABLESPOONS MINCED ITALIAN PARSLEY

¼ CUP FRESHLY GRATED PARMESAN CHEESE

SERVES 4

Heat butter and 2 tablespoons olive oil in a large saucepan over moderate heat. Add onion and saute until soft and sweet, about 10 minutes. Add cabbage, season with salt and pepper, and toss to coat with seasonings. Cover and cook until cabbage is tender, about 15 minutes. Check occasionally to make sure it is not burning; adjust heat accordingly.

Bring broth-water mixture to a simmer in a saucepan and adjust heat to keep it barely simmering. Uncover pot with cabbage and raise heat to moderately high. Add rice and cook, stirring, until rice is hot throughout. Add wine and cook, stirring, until wine is absorbed. Begin adding hot broth ½ cup at a time, stirring frequently and waiting until each addition has been absorbed before adding more. Adjust heat so that mixture simmers gently, not vigorously. It should take 20 to 22 minutes for the rice to become al dente—firm to the tooth but with no hard core. The mixture should be creamy—neither soupy nor stiff. You may not need all the liquid; if you need a little more, use boiling water.

When rice is done, add remaining tablespoon olive oil, ¼ teaspoon lemon zest, the parsley and the cheese. Stir vigorously, then taste and adjust seasoning. You may want to add a little more lemon zest, but the lemon flavor should be subtle. Divide risotto among 4 warm bowls.

braised red cabbage with pears

Somehow a shiny red cabbage from the farmers' market, its wrapper leaves still attached, is much more inspiring than its grocery-store counterpart. With a small head, or half a large one, and a single pear, you can prepare a delicate sweet-and-sour red cabbage. The grated pear dissolves and virtually disappears in the braised cabbage, contributing a gentle sweetness. Serve with pork, rabbit, duck or game.

¾ POUND RED CABBAGE, IN 2 OR 3 WEDGES, CORED

1 LARGE BOSC OR BARTLETT PEAR (8 TO 10 OUNCES)

2 TABLESPOONS UNSALTED BUTTER, IN SMALL PIECES

2 TABLESPOONS BALSAMIC VINEGAR, OR MORE TO TASTE

SALT AND FRESHLY GROUND BLACK PEPPER

SERVES 4

Slice the cabbage wedges finely by hand. Transfer to a pot. Quarter, core and peel the pear. Grate the pear on the coarse side of a four-sided grater. Add to the pot along with the butter, 2 tablespoons balsamic vinegar, and salt and pepper to taste. Cover and cook over moderately low heat, stirring often, until cabbage is tender, about 30 minutes. Taste and adjust seasoning, adding another splash of balsamic vinegar if necessary.

steamed mussels with celery root and aioli

These mussels are definitely finger food. Using the shells as a spoon, you can accompany every mussel with little bits of aromatic vegetables and aioli-enriched broth. At the market, choose a small celery root so you won't have any left over. Once cut, it's not a great keeper because it quickly discolors. If you must buy a larger celery root, cut it in half and peel only the half you will use for this recipe. Rub the cut side of the other half with lemon, wrap tightly and refrigerate for use the next day in vegetable soup or a potato-celery root puree.

¼ CUP OLIVE OIL

⅓ CUP MINCED SHALLOTS

2 CARROTS, IN ¼-INCH DICE

2 CELERY RIBS, IN ¼-INCH DICE

1 SMALL CELERY ROOT, THICKLY PEELED, IN ¼-INCH DICE

3 CLOVES GARLIC, MINCED

SALT AND FRESHLY GROUND BLACK PEPPER

1 CUP DRY WHITE WINE

3 TABLESPOONS MINCED ITALIAN PARSLEY

2 POUNDS SMALL MUSSELS, DEBEARDED AND SCRUBBED CLEAN, TIGHTLY CLOSED

½ CUP AIOLI (PAGE 110)

SERVES 4 AS A MAIN COURSE, 6 AS A FIRST COURSE

Heat olive oil in a large pot over moderate heat. Add shallots, carrots, celery, celery root and garlic. Season with salt and pepper. Saute vegetables until soft, 10 to 12 minutes. Add wine, 2 tablespoons parsley and mussels. Raise heat to high and bring to a simmer. Cover and cook, shaking pot occasionally, until the mussels open and the raw wine taste has dissipated, about 5 minutes. Discard any mussels that do not open.

Put aioli in a small bowl and whisk in enough of the mussel liquor to make a sauce thin enough to drizzle. Divide mussels among warm bowls. Spoon the vegetables and juices over them. Drizzle with aioli. Garnish with the remaining parsley.

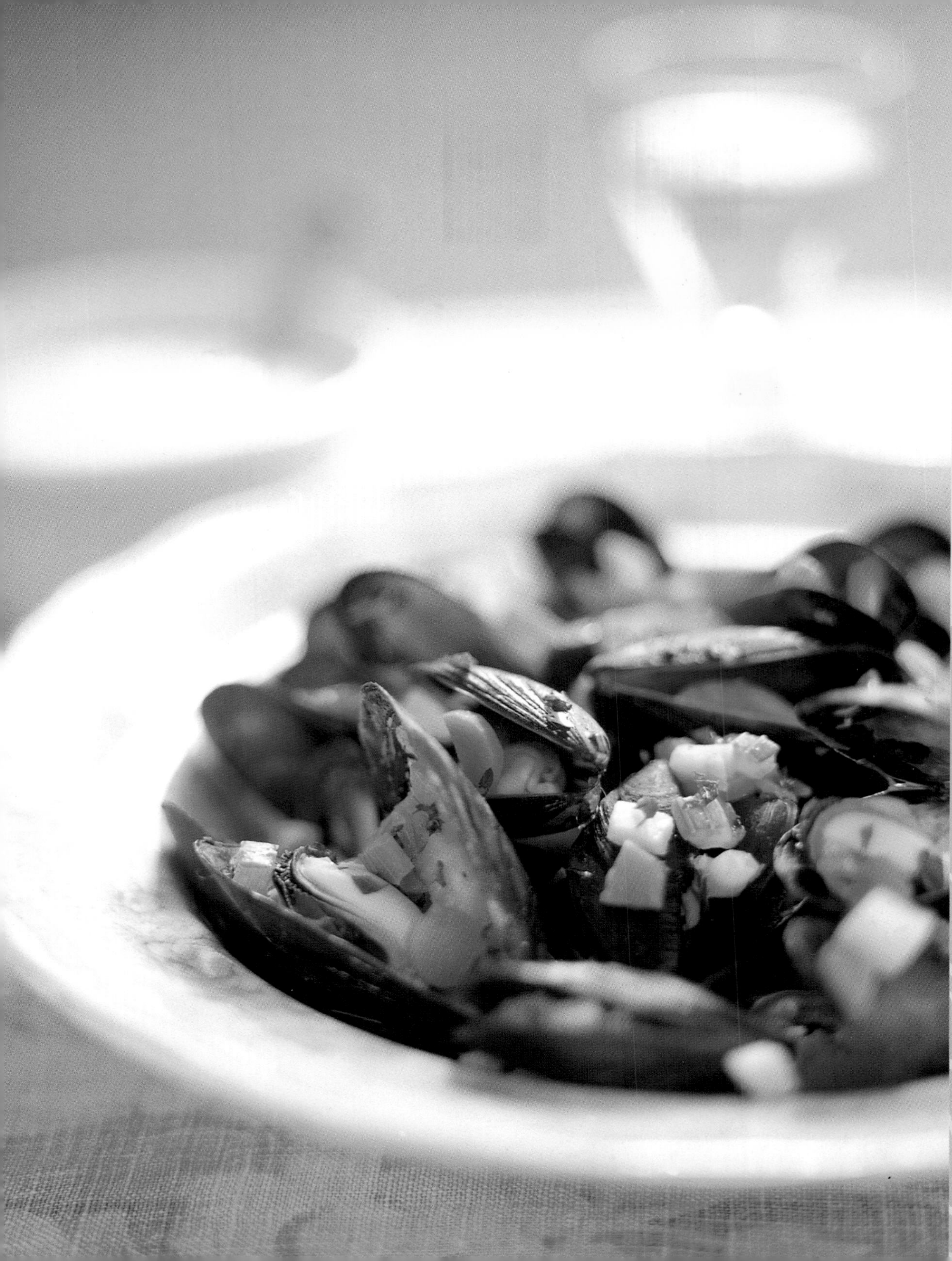

blood orange compote

I wish more Americans had the habit of offering fresh fruit at the end of the meal instead of a rich dessert. Especially after a big dinner, a bowl of ripe pears or a fruit compote is much more appealing to me than pastry. When you can find heavy, sweet blood oranges at the farmers' market, make this beautiful compote and see if you don't find it perfectly satisfying. The blood oranges tint the spiced syrup an appetizing raspberry red.

5 LARGE OR 6 MEDIUM BLOOD
ORANGES
¼ CUP SUGAR
1 CUP DRY WHITE WINE
1 CINNAMON STICK
1 WHOLE CLOVE
2 SLICES PEELED FRESH GINGER,
EACH ABOUT THE SIZE OF A
QUARTER AND ¼ INCH THICK

SERVES 6

With a sharp vegetable peeler, remove four wide strips of zest—orange part only, no white pith—from 1 of the oranges. Set aside.

Cut a slice off both ends of each orange so it will stand upright. Stand each orange on a cutting surface and, using a sharp knife, remove all the peel and white pith by slicing from top to bottom all the way around the orange, following the contour of the fruit. Slice peeled oranges crosswise ¼ inch thick. Discard the first and last slices if they seem to be mostly membranes. Remove the small bit of white pith at the center of each slice. Arrange fruit in a serving bowl (preferably glass or crystal) in layers.

In a saucepan, combine sugar, wine, cinnamon stick, clove, orange zest and 1 cup water. Smash the ginger with the flat side of a large knife and add it to the saucepan. Bring to a simmer over moderate heat, stirring to dissolve sugar. Adjust heat to maintain a simmer and cook until mixture is reduced to 1½ cups, about 10 minutes. Strain syrup to remove spices and zest. Pour hot syrup over oranges. Cool to room temperature, then cover and chill for several hours or overnight.

To serve, divide oranges and syrup among 6 serving bowls.

orange and dried cranberry compote: Substitute navel oranges for the blood oranges. Add ½ cup dried cranberries, sprinkling them between the orange layers. Over the course of several hours, the cranberries will tinge the syrup a pretty rose.

orecchiette with chard and ricotta salata

The southern Italian region of Apulia, where orecchiette ("little ears") are a specialty, is the nation's garden, source of much of its produce. Small wonder, then, that pasta-and-vegetable dishes abound there and that orecchiette's usual companion is a vegetable sauce—orecchiette with cauliflower; with tomato sauce and aged ricotta; or, most famously, with broccoli rabe.

This variation on the region's signature dish uses chard in place of broccoli rabe. Other sturdy greens you find at the farmers' market could stand in for the chard. However, if they are at all tough or strong tasting, blanch them first, instead of steaming them as indicated for the chard.

2 BUNCHES GREEN CHARD, ABOUT 14 OUNCES EACH

⅓ CUP PLUS 1 TABLESPOON EXTRA VIRGIN OLIVE OIL

6 CLOVES GARLIC, THINLY SLICED

¼ TEASPOON HOT RED PEPPER FLAKES

SALT AND FRESHLY GROUND BLACK PEPPER

1 POUND DRIED ORECCHIETTE

4 OUNCES RICOTTA SALATA CHEESE

184

SERVES 4 TO 6

Separate chard leaves from ribs with a knife. Reserve the ribs for another use. (One idea: Cut ribs in small pieces, boil until tender, then reheat in olive oil with garlic and dust with Parmesan cheese.) Wash the leaves in a sinkful of water and lift them out of the water into a colander. Transfer to a large pot with just the water clinging to them. Cover and cook over moderate heat until wilted, about 5 minutes. Drain, pressing out excess water, but don't squeeze them dry. Chop coarsely.

Heat ⅓ cup olive oil in a 12-inch skillet over moderate heat. Add garlic and hot-pepper flakes and saute until garlic is lightly colored, about 2 minutes. Add greens, season highly with salt and pepper and toss to coat with seasonings. Keep warm.

Bring a large pot of salted water to a boil over high heat. Add pasta and cook until al dente. Drain, reserving ½ cup of the cooking water. Return pasta to pot and add remaining tablespoon oil. Toss until coated, then add greens and toss again. Grate ricotta salata over the pasta and toss again gently, adding a little of the reserved water if needed to keep pasta moist. Transfer to warm plates.

braised chard with chick-peas

As appealing as barely wilted chard leaves are as a salad, slow cooking transforms them into something arguably even more savory. Braised with onions, garlic and chick-peas, the chard develops a deep, earthy flavor that would complement baked tuna, pork chops or sausage. Chard is not as frost-hardy as some other greens, such as collards and kale; if you can't find it in your winter market, you can substitute kale, but it may need to cook longer. Look for Red Russian kale or other tender flat-leaved varieties that have a texture comparable to chard's. Curly kale, being tougher, should probably be blanched before using it here.

2 BUNCHES GREEN CHARD, ABOUT 14 OUNCES EACH

3 TABLESPOONS EXTRA VIRGIN OLIVE OIL

2 CLOVES GARLIC, MINCED

½ MEDIUM ONION, MINCED

PINCH HOT RED PEPPER FLAKES

1 CAN (15½ OUNCES) CHICK-PEAS, DRAINED AND RINSED

SALT

1½ TEASPOONS FRESH LEMON JUICE, OR MORE TO TASTE

SERVES 6

Separate chard leaves from ribs; reserve ribs for another use (see page 184) or discard. You should have about 1 pound leaves. Wash the leaves in a sinkful of water, lift them out and drain well in a colander. Stack the leaves a few at a time and slice crosswise into ¼-inch-wide ribbons. Set aside.

Heat olive oil in a 12-inch skillet over moderate heat. Add garlic and onion and saute until onion is soft, 5 to 10 minutes. Add hot-pepper flakes and saute 1 minute to release their character. Add chick-peas and stir to coat with seasonings. Add chard leaves, season well with salt and stir to blend. The leaves are bulky and you may need to add them in batches, letting them cook down slightly before adding more. Cook, stirring, until the leaves have wilted enough that you can cover the skillet. Cover, adjust heat to maintain a gentle simmer and cook until chard is tender, about 15 minutes. Remove from heat and stir in 1½ teaspoons lemon juice.

Serve warm or at room temperature, not hot. Taste and adjust seasoning just before serving.

warm dandelion and bacon salad

Supermarkets rarely carry dandelion greens at all, much less greens that are young and tender enough for this salad. But growers who sell at the farmers' market know they have discriminating customers who appreciate the delicate nature of young greens. For this salad, which is "cooked" briefly in the retained warmth of a hot bacon dressing, you need greens that taste good when raw—mild and not too peppery. They should feel tender and have thin stems.

¾ POUND SMALL, YOUNG DANDE-LION GREENS

2 LARGE EGGS

1 ½ TABLESPOONS MAYONNAISE

½ TABLESPOON CAPERS, COARSELY CHOPPED

1 ½ TABLESPOONS THINLY SLICED FRESH CHIVES

SALT AND FRESHLY GROUND BLACK PEPPER

8 SLICES BAGUETTE OR OTHER COUNTRY-STYLE BREAD, EACH ABOUT ½ INCH THICK AND 3 INCHES LONG

4 THICK SLICES BACON, SLICED CROSSWISE IN ½-INCH-WIDE PIECES

2 TABLESPOONS RED WINE VIN-EGAR, OR MORE AS NEEDED

SERVES 4

Wash the dandelion greens, discarding any bruised ones and any thick stems. Tear any large leaves in half or thirds. Dry thoroughly in a salad spinner. You should have about ½ pound trimmed greens. Save any extra for another salad. Place dandelion greens in a large bowl.

Put eggs in a small saucepan with cold water to cover. Bring to a boil over moderately high heat, then cover and set aside for 10 minutes. Drain and cool under cold running water, then peel and chop coarsely. Transfer eggs to a small bowl and stir in mayonnaise, capers, 1 tablespoon chives, and salt and pepper to taste.

Toast bread on both sides under a broiler or in a toaster. Top each toast with some of the egg salad, sprinkle with some of the remaining chives and set aside.

Saute bacon in a 10-inch skillet over moderately low heat until it releases much of its fat and just begins to crisp. Transfer bacon and fat to the bowl with the dandelion greens. With skillet off heat, add 2 tablespoons wine vinegar to skillet. Stir quickly with a wooden spoon to release any flavorful bits clinging to the bottom of the skillet, then pour over salad. Toss well. Season to taste with salt and pepper and more vinegar if needed. Toss again. Transfer to a serving bowl. Pass toasts separately.

white bean soup with winter greens

Adding a swirl of winter greens makes this white bean soup almost a meal in itself. At my house, we might have a platter of sliced prosciutto first, with celery hearts, olives and good bread. After the soup: a piece of cheese and some winter fruit.

1 POUND DRIED CANNELLINI OR OTHER WHITE BEANS

¼ CUP EXTRA VIRGIN OLIVE OIL, PLUS MORE FOR GARNISH

1 LARGE ONION, CHOPPED

2 CARROTS, IN ⅓-INCH DICE

4 CLOVES GARLIC, MINCED

3 TABLESPOONS MINCED ITALIAN PARSLEY

2 BAY LEAVES

4 CUPS HOMEMADE OR CANNED LOW-SODIUM CHICKEN BROTH

SALT AND FRESHLY GROUND BLACK PEPPER

¾ POUND WINTER GREENS SUCH AS KALE, CHARD, DANDELION, COLLARD OR TURNIP GREENS

FRESHLY GRATED PARMESAN CHEESE

SERVES 6

Use whatever greens the farmers' market provides in good condition, although I would avoid peppery mustard greens. Flavorful beans also make a difference. If you have access to some of the old-fashioned varieties, you might want to try them here. I found European Soldier beans made a particularly tasty soup.

Soak beans 8 hours or overnight in water to cover by 1 inch. Drain.

Heat ¼ cup olive oil in a large pot over moderate heat. Add onion, carrots, garlic, parsley and bay leaves. Saute until vegetables are slightly softened, about 10 minutes.

Add drained beans, the chicken broth and 2 cups water. Season with salt and pepper. Bring to a simmer, cover and adjust heat to maintain a bare simmer. Cook, stirring occasionally, until beans are tender, 45 minutes to 1½ hours, depending on age of beans. Remove the bay leaves. In a food processor or blender, puree 4 cups of the beans and vegetables with some of their liquid. Return the puree to the pot and stir well. If needed, thin soup with water.

Wash greens well, removing any bruised leaves, thick ribs or stems that are thick or tough. You should have about ½ pound trimmed greens. Stack leaves a few at a time, roll into a log and slice crosswise into ¼-inch-wide ribbons. Bring a large pot of salted water to a boil over high heat. Add greens and boil until tender—a couple of minutes for young dandelion and turnip greens, longer for kale or collard greens. Drain, reserving about 2 cups of the cooking liquid. Stir greens into soup. Cover and simmer an additional 5 minutes. Thin soup, if needed, with reserved cooking liquid. Taste and adjust seasoning.

Serve in warm bowls, topping each portion with a drizzle of olive oil and a sprinkle of cheese.

baked leeks with cream and tarragon

Cooks used to have to throw away about two-thirds of every leek because the tender white and pale green shank was so short. Now breeders have given us leeks with much longer shanks, dramatically increasing the edible portion. For this recipe, check the farmers' market for leeks with a shank about 6 inches long, a size that fits in most baking dishes and is not too large to serve whole. By the end of the baking time, they will be bathed in a creamy tarragon sauce. Serve as a separate first course or as an accompaniment to roast chicken, pork or beef.

8 LEEKS, EACH ABOUT ¾ INCH IN DIAMETER
½ CUP HEAVY CREAM
½ CUP HOMEMADE OR CANNED LOW-SODIUM CHICKEN BROTH
1½ TEASPOONS DIJON MUSTARD
1 TEASPOON MINCED FRESH TARRAGON
SALT AND FRESHLY GROUND BLACK PEPPER

188

SERVES 4

Preheat oven to 375 degrees F. Cut off the dark green leek tops, leaving only the white and pale green shank. Trim the root end but leave the base intact to hold the leek together. Slit the leeks lengthwise, stopping about 2 inches short of the base. Rinse well between the layers to dislodge any dirt. Arrange leeks in a shallow baking dish just large enough to hold them in one layer.

In a small bowl, whisk together cream, broth, mustard, tarragon and salt and pepper to taste. Pour over leeks. Bake 30 minutes, then turn leeks over with tongs. Return to oven and bake until leeks have absorbed almost all the creamy sauce and have begun to brown on top, 35 to 45 more minutes. Serve hot or warm.

whipped parsnips and potatoes

Even among the vegetable lovers who shop at farmers' markets, parsnips often get the cold shoulder. Growers tell me they can bring a mere 20 pounds to market, and go home with half that. It's a shame, because people would surely appreciate parsnips' nutty sweet potatolike flavor if they would give them a try. Pureed with potatoes and chives, they lend a gentle root-vegetable sweetness. If you don't have a food mill, quarter the parsnips lengthwise and remove the core before boiling, then whip them with the potatoes, butter and cream in an electric mixer. Serve the smooth puree with roast pork, roast duck or a Christmas prime rib.

1 POUND PARSNIPS
¾ POUND BAKING POTATOES
½ CUP HEAVY CREAM
2 SHALLOTS, MINCED
1 TABLESPOON THINLY SLICED
FRESH CHIVES
2 TABLESPOONS UNSALTED BUTTER
SALT AND FRESHLY GROUND
BLACK PEPPER

SERVES 6

Peel parsnips and potatoes and cut into ½-inch chunks. Bring a large pot of salted water to a boil over high heat. Add parsnips and potatoes and cook until tender, 8 to 10 minutes. While vegetables are boiling, combine cream, shallots and chives in a small saucepan and bring to a simmer; simmer 1 minute, then adjust heat to keep warm without simmering.

Drain parsnips and potatoes in a sieve and shake dry. Position a food mill over the warm dry pot the vegetables were boiled in. Pass the vegetables through the mill directly into the pot. With a wooden spoon, beat in butter and warm cream mixture. Season well with salt and pepper. Serve immediately.

turkey soup with root vegetables

While you are buying your Thanksgiving sweet potatoes and brussels sprouts at the farmers' market, don't forget a few root vegetables for the day-after-Thanksgiving soup. At my house, the turkey leftovers are held in high esteem, and the postholiday menu never varies: thick turkey sandwiches for lunch, and for dinner a vegetable soup made with parsnips, carrots, rutabagas and the leftover carcass. I add orzo, the rice-shaped pasta, but any small pasta shape will do. The soup's simplicity always appeals after Thanksgiving's excess.

FOR THE TURKEY BROTH:

1 ROAST TURKEY CARCASS OR 3 TO 4 POUNDS TURKEY NECKS, BACKS AND WINGS
3 CELERY RIBS, CHOPPED
2 CARROTS, CHOPPED
1 ONION, CHOPPED
¼ BUNCH ITALIAN PARSLEY
2 BAY LEAVES
1 DOZEN BLACK PEPPERCORNS
SALT

FOR THE SOUP:

2 TABLESPOONS OLIVE OIL
1 ONION, CHOPPED
2 CELERY RIBS, IN ⅓-INCH DICE
2 CARROTS, IN ⅓-INCH DICE
1 LARGE OR 2 SMALL PARSNIPS, QUARTERED LENGTHWISE, CORES REMOVED, IN ⅓-INCH DICE
½ POUND RUTABAGA, THICKLY PEELED, IN ⅓-INCH DICE
2 CLOVES GARLIC, MINCED
2 TABLESPOONS MINCED ITALIAN PARSLEY
SALT AND FRESHLY GROUND BLACK PEPPER
1 CUP ORZO
FRESHLY GRATED PARMESAN CHEESE, OPTIONAL

SERVES 6

To make the turkey broth: With a heavy knife or cleaver, chop the turkey carcass into 3 or 4 pieces that will fit in a large pot. Transfer the pieces to the pot and add 3 quarts cold water. Bring to a boil over moderate heat, skimming any scum that collects on the surface. Add celery, carrots, onion, parsley, bay leaves and peppercorns. Adjust heat to maintain a gentle simmer and cook 3 hours. Cool to room temperature, then strain. Set aside 8 cups, reserving any remaining broth for another use.

To make the soup: Heat olive oil in large pot over moderate heat. Add onion and saute until softened, about 10 minutes. Add celery, carrots, parsnips and rutabaga and saute about 5 minutes longer. Add garlic and parsley and saute 1 minute to release garlic fragrance. Add reserved 8 cups turkey broth, bring to a simmer, season with salt and pepper and cover partially. Adjust heat to maintain a simmer and cook until vegetables are barely tender, about 15 minutes. Stir in orzo and cook until it is barely done, about 7 minutes. Cover, remove from heat and let stand 5 minutes.

Taste and adjust seasoning. Ladle into warm soup bowls. Pass Parmesan cheese at the table, if desired.

winter garden pasta

This flexible southern Italian sauce can be built around whatever winter greens you find at the market. The greens are chopped rather fine, then braised until tender with anchovy, rosemary and garlic. I first had such a pasta sauce in the mountainous Molise region of Italy, made by a cook who told me his version contained chard, spinach, escarole, broccoli rabe and a little cauliflower. I've also used dandelion greens, turnip greens and broccoli florets. A mixture of at least three different vegetables gives the most interesting results. Avoid sturdy greens, such as kale or collards, which take longer to cook.

7 TABLESPOONS EXTRA VIRGIN OLIVE OIL

½ ONION, MINCED

4 CLOVES GARLIC, MINCED

4 ANCHOVIES, MINCED

2 TABLESPOONS CHOPPED CAPERS

2 TABLESPOONS CHOPPED NIÇOISE OLIVES

1½ POUNDS MIXED WINTER GREENS (SEE RECIPE INTRODUCTION), COARSE STEMS OR RIBS REMOVED, THEN CHOPPED MEDIUM-FINE

1 FRESH ROSEMARY SPRIG, 4 INCHES LONG

SALT AND FRESHLY GROUND BLACK PEPPER

1 POUND DRIED ORECCHIETTE, CAVATELLI OR FUSILLI

½ CUP FRESHLY GRATED PECORINO ROMANO CHEESE

SERVES 6

Heat 5 tablespoons olive oil in a 12-inch skillet over moderate heat. Add onion and saute until soft and sweet, about 10 minutes. Add garlic and anchovies and saute 1 minute to release garlic fragrance. Add capers and olives and saute 1 minute. Add greens, rosemary sprig, and salt and pepper to taste. Stir to coat with seasonings. Cover and cook until greens are tender and flavorful, 20 to 30 minutes. Uncover and stir occasionally, and adjust heat as necessary so greens don't stick. Remove rosemary sprig when the rosemary flavor is as strong as you like; it should be subtle.

Bring a large pot of salted water to a boil over high heat. Add pasta and cook until al dente. Drain and return to pot. Add remaining 2 tablespoons oil and toss to coat. Add greens and all but 2 tablespoons cheese. Toss well. Divide pasta among 6 warm plates. Sprinkle remaining cheese on top.

notes

notes

notes

notes

resources

Any list of farmers' markets would be out-of-date soon after printing. Markets constantly open and close, or change locations and hours. To find markets in your area, or in an area you plan to visit, contact the appropriate state department of agriculture. Direct-marketing specialists within these departments often have current information about markets in their state. County extension agents are another good information source.

Other resources for market locations include:

United States Department of Agriculture
Agricultural Marketing Service
202-720-8317
www.ams.usda.gov/farmersmarkets/map.htm
The USDA's Agricultural Marketing Service provides support for farmers' markets nationwide. Resources available from the USDA include a list of farmers' markets by state and region as well as a farmers' market resource guide.

Resources for Farmers' Markets
www.farmersmarketsusa.org/
A Web site linking farmers' market vendors, market managers and consumers; includes farm profiles, a directory of farmers' markets nationwide, and a list of regional market associations.

The following organizations may be of interest to those who care about the future of farmers' markets in America:

American Farmland Trust
1200 18th Street, NW
Suite 800
Washington, DC 20036
202-331-7300
www.farmland.org/
Dedicated to preserving America's agricultural resources, the nonprofit American Farmland Trust helps rescue farms endangered by development and encourages sustainable farming practices.

Community Alliance with Family Farmers
P.O. Box 363
Davis, CA 95617
530-756-8518
www.caff.org/
CAFF's mission is to build a movement of rural and urban people to foster family-scale agriculture that cares for the land, sustains local economies, and promotes social justice.

Project for Public Spaces, Inc.
The Public Market Collaborative
700 Broadway, 4th Floor
New York, NY 10003
212-620-5660
www.pps.org/info/projects/markets_projects/
The Collaborative helps establish and preserve public markets by providing technical assistance and educational programs in market development, design and operation.

bibliography

The following books and catalogs have been helpful to me in preparing this manuscript.

BOOKS

Blanc, Georges. *The Natural Cuisine of Georges Blanc*. New York: Stewart, Tabori & Chang, 1987.

Carcione, Joe, and Bob Lucas. *The Greengrocer*. San Francisco: Chronicle Books, 1972.

Creasy, Rosalind. *The Complete Book of Edible Landscaping*. San Francisco: Sierra Club Books, 1982.

Field, Carol. *The Italian Baker*. New York: Harper & Row, 1985.

Giobbi, Edward. *Pleasures of the Good Earth*. New York: Alfred A. Knopf, 1991.

La Place, Viana. *Verdura: Vegetables Italian Style*. New York: William Morrow, 1991.

Lucas, Dione. *The Cordon Bleu Cook Book*. Boston: Little, Brown and Company, 1947.

Margen, Sheldon, M.D., and the Editors of the University of California at Berkeley Wellness Letter. *The Wellness Encyclopedia of Food and Nutrition*. New York: Rebus, 1992.

Morash, Marian. *The Victory Garden Cookbook*. New York: Alfred A. Knopf, 1982.

Morganti, Paolo. *Il radicchio rosso di Treviso*. Treviso: Morganti Editore, 1994.

National Gardening Association. *Gardening: The Complete Guide to Growing America's Favorite Fruits & Vegetables*. Reading: Addison-Wesley Publishing Company, 1986.

Root, Waverley. *Food*. New York: Simon & Schuster, 1980.

Schneider, Elizabeth. *Uncommon Fruits & Vegetables, A Commonsense Guide*. New York: Harper & Row, 1986.

Shere, Lindsey R. *Chez Panisse Desserts*. New York: Random House, 1985.

Spitzer, Theodore Morrow, and Hilary Baum. *Public Markets and Community Revitalization*. Washington, D.C.: ULI—Urban Land Institute and Project for Public Spaces, Inc., 1995.

CATALOGS

The Cook's Garden, Londonderry, Vermont, 1996.
Johnny's Selected Seeds, Albion, Maine, 1996.
Nichol's Garden Nursery, Albany, Oregon, 1991.
Seeds Blüm, Boise, Idaho, 1996.
Shepherd's Garden Seeds, Felton, California, 1996.
Territorial Seed Company, Cottage Grove, Oregon, 1996.

index

table of equivalents

The exact equivalents in the following tables have been rounded for convenience.

US/UK
OZ=OUNCE
LB=POUND
IN=INCH
FT=FOOT
TBL=TABLESPOON
FL OZ=FLUID OUNCE
QT=QUART

Metric
G=GRAM
KG=KILOGRAM
MM=MILLIMETER
CM=CENTIMETER
ML=MILLILITER
L=LITER

Weights

US/UK	METRIC
1 OZ	30 G
2 OZ	60 G
3 OZ	90 G
4 OZ (¼ LB)	125 G
5 OZ (⅓ LB)	155 G
6 OZ	185 G
7 OZ	220 G
8 OZ (½ LB)	250 G
10 OZ	315 G
12 OZ (¾ LB)	375 G
14 OZ	440 G
16 OZ (1 LB)	500 G
1½ LB	750 G
2 LB	1 KG
3 LB	1½ KG

Oven Temperatures

FAHRENHEIT	CELSIUS	GAS
250	120	½
275	140	1
300	150	2
325	160	3
350	180	4
375	190	5
400	200	6
425	220	7
450	230	8
475	240	9
500	260	10

Liquids

US	METRIC	UK
2 TBL	30 ML	1 FL OZ
¼ CUP	60 ML	2 FL OZ
⅓ CUP	80 ML	3 FL OZ
½ CUP	125 ML	4 FL OZ
⅔ CUP	160 ML	5 FL OZ
¾ CUP	180 ML	6 FL OZ
1 CUP	250 ML	8 FL OZ
1½ CUPS	375 ML	12 FL OZ
2 CUPS	500 ML	16 FL OZ

Length Measures

US/UK	METRIC
⅛ IN	3 MM
¼ IN	6 MM
½ IN	12 MM
1 IN	2.5 CM
2 IN	5 CM
3 IN	7.5 CM
4 IN	10 CM
5 IN	13 CM
6 IN	15 CM
7 IN	18 CM
8 IN	20 CM
9 IN	23 CM
10 IN	25 CM
11 IN	28 CM
12 IN/1 FT	30 CM

Equivalents for Commonly Used Ingredients

ALL-PURPOSE (PLAIN) FLOUR/
DRIED BREAD CRUMBS/CHOPPED NUTS

¼ CUP	1 OZ	30 G
⅓ CUP	1½ OZ	45 G
½ CUP	2 OZ	60 G
¾ CUP	3 OZ	90 G
1 CUP	4 OZ	125 G
1½ CUPS	6 OZ	185 G
2 CUPS	8 OZ	250 G

WHOLE-WHEAT (WHOLE MEAL) FLOUR

3 TBL	1 OZ	30 G
½ CUP	2 OZ	60 G
⅔ CUP	3 OZ	90 G
1 CUP	4 OZ	125 G
1¼ CUPS	5 OZ	155 G
1⅔ CUPS	7 OZ	210 G
1¾ CUPS	8 OZ	250 G

BROWN SUGAR

¼ CUP	1½ OZ	45 G
½ CUP	3 OZ	90 G
¾ CUP	4 OZ	125 G
1 CUP	5½ OZ	170 G
1½ CUPS	8 OZ	250 G
2 CUPS	10 OZ	315 G

WHITE SUGAR

¼ CUP	2 OZ	60 G
⅓ CUP	3 OZ	90 G
½ CUP	4 OZ	125 G
¾ CUP	6 OZ	185 G
1 CUP	8 OZ	250 G
1½ CUPS	12 OZ	375 G
2 CUPS	1 LB	500 G

RAISINS/CURRANTS/SEMOLINA

¼ CUP	1 OZ	30 G
⅓ CUP	2 OZ	60 G
½ CUP	3 OZ	90 G
¾ CUP	4 OZ	125 G
1 CUP	5 OZ	155 G

LONG-GRAIN RICE/CORNMEAL

⅓ CUP	2 OZ	60 G
½ CUP	2½ OZ	75 G
¾ CUP	4 OZ	125 G
1 CUP	5 OZ	155 G
1½ CUPS	8 OZ	250 G

DRIED BEANS

¼ CUP	1½ OZ	45 G
⅓ CUP	2 OZ	60 G
½ CUP	3 OZ	90 G
¾ CUP	5 OZ	155 G
1 CUP	6 OZ	185 G
1¼ CUPS	8 OZ	250 G
1½ CUPS	12 OZ	375 G

ROLLED OATS

⅓ CUP	1 OZ	30 G
⅔ CUP	2 OZ	60 G
1 CUP	3 OZ	90 G
1½ CUPS	4 OZ	125 G
2 CUPS	5 OZ	155 G

JAM/HONEY

2 TBL	2 OZ	60 G
¼ CUP	3 OZ	90 G
½ CUP	5 OZ	155 G
¾ CUP	8 OZ	250 G
1 CUP	11 OZ	345 G

GRATED PARMESAN/ROMANO CHEESE

¼ CUP	1 OZ	30 G
½ CUP	2 OZ	60 G
¾ CUP	3 OZ	90 G
1 CUP	4 OZ	125 G
1⅓ CUPS	5 OZ	155 G
2 CUPS	7 OZ	220 G

acknowledgments

This book required the input, advice and assistance of many people, whom I would like to thank here. First, I feel deeply indebted to Sibella Kraus and Lynn Bagley, who have worked tirelessly to revive the tradition of farmers' markets in the San Francisco Bay Area. The markets they established have nurtured many quality-conscious small farms and have made food shopping a year-round pleasure for me and countless others.

Judy Blue at the Ferry Plaza Farmers' Market, Dutch Watazychyn at the Marin County Farmers' Market and Mark Wall of the Southland Farmers' Market Association helped put me in touch with many farmers' market growers. I would also like to thank Joel Patraker of the Greenmarket Farmers Market and Donald Horn of the Lancaster Central Market for taking time to share their markets with me.

For generously sharing recipes, I would like to thank Mary Evely of Simi Winery, Paul Ferrari of Ultra Lucca Delicatessens, Philippe Jeanty of Domaine Chandon, Ann Walker, Susan Walter of Ristorante Ecco and the staff of The Pasta Shop. My thanks to photographer Victoria Pearson, food stylist Janet Miller and designer Clive Piercy for making this a beautiful and inviting book that will, I hope, seduce people into a farmers' market habit. I am also grateful to the staff at Chronicle Books, and especially to Bill LeBlond and Leslie Jonath, for allowing me to do a book on a topic dear to me. And I would particularly like to acknowledge Sharon Silva for her thoughtful, careful and sensitive editing.

The following farmers provided valuable information about the crops they take to market: Frances Andrews, Eat Well Farms; Nick Atallah, Madison Growers; Kathleen Barsotti, Capay Fruits & Vegetables; Tim Bates, The Apple Farm; Mary Ann Carpenter, Coastal Organics; Alex Causey, Briar Patch Farms; Jim Cochran, Swanton Berry Farm; Christine Coke, Coke Farm; Wallace Condon, Small Potatoes; Al Courchesne, Frog

Hollow Farm; Stan Cutter, Cutter Farms; Stan Devoto, Devoto Gardens; Leonard Diggs, Leonard Diggs Organic Farms; Gene Etheridge, Etheridge Farms; Wayne Ferrari, Ferrari Farms; Dave Fredericks, Genuine Exotic Melons; Molly Gean, Iwamoto-Gean; Andy Griffin, Happy Boy Farms; Gary Hamaguchi, Hamada Farms; Jim Hammond, Hazel Dell Mushrooms; Paul Holmes, Terra Firma; Debbie Hurley, Summer Harvest Farms; Tsugio Imamoto; Doreen Lum, Vegetable Patch; Marcia Muzzi; Bob Polito, Polito Family Farms; Ted Richardson, Gabriel Farm; Dru Rivers, Full Belly Farms; Peter Rudnick, Green Gulch Farm; Ignacio Sanchez, Twin Girls Farm; Lou Solari, Solari Ranch; Sue Temple, Fiddler's Green Farm; Sue Verdi, Verdi's Farm-Fresh Produce; Parker Watwood, Jolon Farms/Millennium Farms; Bud Weisenberg, Green Hills Farm; and Denesse Willey, T. & D. Willey Farms.

Finally, I must thank my husband Doug for being willing to stop at a farmers' market anywhere, anytime, and for his good-natured participation in all my projects.

FROM THE MARKET

FRESH

FROM THE

FARMER'S

MARKET

FRESH